A Tropical Adventure in the 1950s

Best Wishes
Gwendoline Page

A Tropical Adventure

in the 1950s

by

Gwendoline Page

Previous books by the same author:

Coconuts and Coral
Growing Pains – A Teenager's War
We Kept The Secret
They Listened In Secret
The Chocolate Elephant

ISBN 9780900616 884

Printed and published by
Geo. R. Reeve Ltd., 9-11 Town Green, Wymondham, Norfolk

CONTENTS

CHAPTER ONE

Introduction

Ever since I can remember, my one over-riding ambition has been to travel.

As a child of eight or nine onwards, I would ignore all those books of noble, but to my mind boring stories of deeds, or misdeeds which took place among the pupils of fictional schools and make for the shelves of adventure, telling the tales of the great explorers of the world. Their exciting journeys, the strange names, the difficulties encountered in remote regions all combined to make me want to be there with them hacking a way through the bush, paddling up a mysterious river, or riding over vast plains.

The last bit about the plains probably caught my imagination about the age of eleven when I remember confiding to a friend that I wanted to be a cow-girl since I could not be a cowboy!

My urge to travel could have been inherited from my forbears. They seem to have been a roving lot. My brother, who also appears to have inherited the urge, met a number of our far-flung relations in various parts of the world when he was serving in the Merchant Navy. Vancouver, Canada, San Pedro, California, Cape Town, South Africa, Sydney and Melbourne, Australia, were all ports where he found family connections.

In the days of Queen Victoria and large families whole sections of our great, great and even great again family had left the coast of England for some distant horizon.

Of my father's family on both his paternal and maternal sides, uncles and aunts had gone to seek pioneering lives in the vast wildernesses of Australia and Canada and most had prospered there.

As a young man my father had the wanderlust and worked his passage to Canada where he found work in Halifax for a while before travelling across the breadth of the country taking various jobs as he went and carrying his accommodation on his back. At different times he worked as a cook in a lumber camp, helped with the round up on a cattle station and with the salmon fishing in British Columbia. It was only the outbreak of the First World War that brought him back to this country by working his passage home via South America.

His sister decided to try India. She went as governess to a doctor's family in Kashmir and spent a number of years in the foothills of the Himalayas.

With this background it was hardly surprising that my brother and I had "itchy feet"!

I was just fourteen, when the Second World War broke out. My ambition seemed doomed and out of the question for some years. Then my parents spoke of sending us out of the war zone to relatives in South Africa. Papers were prepared, medical tests were taken and we were all ready to leave when a ship carrying hundreds of British children to North America was sunk by enemy action and many of the children were drowned. That was the last that we heard from Mother and Father about being evacuated. We would all take our chances with the bombs at home.

They certainly did not expect to find the war still raging by the time I was eighteen. But it was, and all eighteen-year-olds had to be prepared to serve either in one of the three forces. In the case of girls it was the ATS or Auxiliary Territorial Service to give it its full title, the WAAF or Women's Auxiliary Air Force, the WRNS, Women's Royal Navy Service, or choose to enrol as a Land Girl or work in a munitions factory. There were some reserved occupations, but these did not appeal to me at all. Now was my opportunity for the great adventure!

At seventeen and a half I volunteered to join the WRNS and having passed all the necessary qualifications was accepted. When my call up papers came, my excitement was intense. To which great port was I destined? What great ships and busy waterways would I see?

I opened the envelope and came down to earth with a bump. Mill Hill was where I was to report, a 'Concrete Freighter' as it is known in the Navy, with not a ship or sailor in sight and only four miles from my home. To say I was disappointed was to put it mildly, but still I hoped for better things to come in time.

My brother had more luck and received orders to join a ship as an apprentice. We left home in the same week, which I suppose was a bit hard on our parents. It was another eighteen months before we were to meet again.

CHAPTER TWO

The Adventure Begins

As I have already written about my time in the WRNS in my book GROWING PAINS-A TEENAGER'S WAR, still available in libraries. I will skip that part except to say that I did not get to a port for some time, but was sent to Bletchley Park in the middle of the country. It was only when the European war came to an end and I was transferred on to Japanese signals that I finally achieved my wish to travel abroad and was sent to Colombo , Ceylon (now Sri Lanka) . Here on this tropical island I first set foot on foreign soil and incidentally met my future husband Harry.

My next venture abroad did not occur until 1954. In the meantime Harry and I had married and produced two daughters. We had both left the Navy and were pursuing teaching careers, mine somewhat part-time and erratic due to the two daughters mentioned.

When I say abroad, I do not include the short two weeks visit to Jersey in the Channel Islands that constituted our honeymoon.

In 1946, post war Britain was still a stark and uncomfortable period of shortages and rationing. Most of the little luxuries of life were missing and people were trying hard to make some return to normality after six years of war. The Channel Islands had been occupied by German Forces and if anything the shortages were probably even greater there. However Jersey in the Channel Islands was where we elected to go. The problem was getting there. Transport was difficult. No air service was in operation at that time so going by sea was the only answer.

We travelled on a ship built originally for the St. Malo run, a smaller vessel than usually used for the longer crossing from Weymouth. I had been warned that the crossing would be rough, but as I had had not the slightest sensation of sea- sickness on my travels to Ceylon and back, I thought I was immune from such things. How wrong can you be?

Travelling at night after an exciting day can be wearisome and there were no berths to be had. Cabins had been unavailable when we booked so we spent the first part of our wedding night walking round the deck of this small crowded vessel.

Eventually my legs gave out and I just had to rest. Harry managed to persuade a steward to find me a deck chair in the large sleeping area allocated to the female sex and their children, while he and another naval officer who had been on destroyers, continued to walk the deck. These two, both in naval uniforms were of the few unaffected by the conflicting currents of the ocean. Most of the other passengers clinging desperately to the rails and contributing their last meal to the fishes.

Meanwhile I settled down to try and get some sleep. It proved to be impossible. Every few seconds the ship vibrated with the thud of a wave on its side, or rose and hesitated before plunging down into a trough with a shudder that shook every part of its innards and mine as well. The upshot was that my immunity failed me and I joined the rest of the passengers in losing the contents of my stomach.

As soon as dawn broke I stumbled up on deck to join Harry in the hope that fresh air would revive me. Harry and his friend of the destroyer were still unaffected by the passage and in good spirits. I could not say I was the same. Nobody ever felt less like a blooming bride than I did.

It appeared the ship was delayed and having to wait off Corbiere lighthouse for the tide to turn before putting into St. Helier port. We could see the lighthouse and surrounding rocks in the distance. It was a hopeful sign and with the coming of daylight the frantic movements of the ship seemed to have moderated a little although the swell of the waves still gave the sensation of a ride on a roller coaster.

When the smell of bacon and eggs cooking reached us from the direction of the galley, my stomach did another turn. Not so Harry's. He just felt hungry. Leaving me to recover in the fresh air. Harry went to get his breakfast. Forty minutes or so later he returned looking somewhat mortified. It appears he had ordered his bacon and eggs and sat down to enjoy it all. He went to the toast and marmalade stage when he felt an urgent need to leave the table. He just made his way to the men's' cloakroom in time, where he lost his entire meal. His only consolation was that at least he did it in private and did not disgrace his uniform!

We later met a woman whose father had sailed the seven seas in a windjammer never once suffering sea- sickness. It was not until he retired to live in the Channel Islands that this fine record was broken! Having heard that story we felt a little mollified.

After the ship docked, we made our way pale and wan to the guesthouse where we were to spend the next two weeks. Having had a wash and brush up we went to the dining room for our first meal. We were each presented with a plate on which reposed a slice of toast and three green sardines! Hardly tactful on the part of the proprietor! It was too much for me. I left the sardines where they were and went to bed for the rest of the morning.

CHAPTER THREE

Return to the Tropics

On to 1954. At this time we were living in our home in the small seaside town of Exmouth in South Devon. It is a delightful place in which to live, beautiful countryside all around and the sea almost on one's doorstep. So why did we move? It was that old gypsy urge again and this time there were two of us with itchy feet!

Harry saw an advertisement for a teaching job with the Air Ministry schools in Malaya. He applied and was accepted. The only snag was that he would be required to fly out ahead of the family who would have to wait until a sea passage was available. We were warned that this might involve a separation time of up to nine months.

Having talked it over we decided to take a chance and one snowy morning in January, the children and I waved a tremulous farewell and Harry flew off to sunnier climes.

The very next morning I received a telegram from the Air Ministry saying that the children and I were booked a passage on a ship leaving from Southampton the following month. Delighted as I was, this involved some fast work on my part. Arrangements for letting our house had to be made, personal items stored away safely, children and self kited out with clothes suitable for a tropical climate, Not easy in mid-winter in those days before the vogue for holidays abroad. However, with the help of a house agent and helpful store in Exeter I managed these things and with the aid of a friend even decorated one of the bedrooms. Most of the children's winter clothes I sold or gave away, just keeping enough to see us though to the sailing date, for we would be away for three years or more and in that time the children would grow in size. Then of course there was the paper work involved, letters to write, forms to fill in, insurance and passports to deal with.

The morning the carrier man came to take the heavy luggage that had to be sent on ahead of us, I was still trying to close the

13

last trunk. According to instructions all luggage had to be marked RAF. I had remembered this that same morning, found some white paint and a brush and on the lid of the trunk painted RAF in large white letters. When the carrier arrived I was having great difficulty in closing this last trunk. He saw my problem and before I could stop him he sat on the lid and forced it down. He succeeded in securing the trunk and stood up. As he turned I saw printed in white on the black cloth of the seat of his trousers, RAF backwards ! I did not have the nerve to tell him.

My parents came down from Sussex to spend the last week with us and to help with the last minute jobs. I had knitted two woolly hats in the brightest of colours for the girls. Each hat had a multi-coloured woollen bobble on its top. This was to enable me to spot them quickly should we become separated.

On February 4th we boarded the train in Exeter station on route for Southampton. Jennifer aged seven carrying her treasured Teddy Bear and Virginia her favourite doll, as her Teddy being on the large size had had to be sent ahead in a trunk. If I was slightly apprehensive about transporting two young children and myself safely to Malaya, there was no need to be. On reaching Southampton station we had only a short wait before a RAF bus arrived to convey us all to the docks where our ship was berthed.

During the waiting period we were befriended by another family, a meteorologist, his wife and children, whom were all travelling out to Singapore. The RAF relieved us of our luggage and left us reasonably unencumbered to deal with customs and boarding formalities. However, when I saw the long queue we had to join and envisaged the long tedious wait involved with two young children, my heart sank.

Fate stepped in with a knight in shining armour. Well, maybe not exactly shining armour, but a customs excise uniform. He quietly came to me and suggested I take the children to sit and wait nearby and he would deal with the formalities for me. He was as good as his word and within a few minutes returned with my passport and embarkation card and we were free to go on board.

Our cabin was above the water line and in reasonably spacious first class accommodation. The children were delighted with the bunks and especially the ladder for climbing to the top one. A wash basin was provided but no toilet so my first task of exploration was to find the bathroom. Luckily it was not far off and having established our position and made sure that we all knew the cabin number, I took the girls back on deck to watch the activities on the dock and wave farewell to England. The ship sailed that afternoon out of Southampton harbour and straight into a winter storm!

The ship pitched and plunged and we were in danger from the unattached furniture, in this case an armchair, which slid from one side of the cabin to the other with every rolling wave confining the three of us to the safety of our bunks. Jennifer was the first to suffer from the dreaded 'Mal de Mer' and Virginia followed soon after. As long as I could lie flat I managed to keep my stomach under control, but it was necessary to get up to see to the children and that caused an upheaval.

A steward did his best to persuade us to eat and drink something, but dry biscuits and a little water were all we could manage. Our weather friend came to see how we were. His family were also laid low. He had safely negotiated the gangways and stairs and our cabin door when the ship gave another plunge. Fred grabbed the nearest item for support that turned out to be the bunk ladder. The ladder came adrift and it and Fred slid full length on the cabin floor.

The storm continued for five days and nights. Not only did we suffer from sea- sickness, but also Jennifer developed an abscess in her ear that caused her a lot of pain and lack of sleep. Luckily the ship's doctor was able to give her some antibiotic tablets that solved the problem fairly quickly.

At last the storm seemed to moderate and the winds eased. I dressed the children warmly and complete with scarves and woolly hats we staggered up on deck to breathe in some fresh air. Having walked twice around the deck, the girls showed signs of recovery and I took them to the dining room for their first meal.

From there on life improved greatly and the children were no worse for their experience. As for me, I found that my clothes went on a lot more easily for about a week, but would not recommend such a drastic means to slimming. By the end of the voyage, having indulged in the excellent meals provided by the chefs on board my figure was back to where it started!

Once into the Mediterranean, the sun shone and the round of entertainment and leisure began. We started to recognise fellow passengers and friendships were made. Port Said was the first port of call. The ship was surrounded by Bum Boats full of intriguing goods for sale, tooled leather handbags, cushions made of camel skin, woven items and small boxes made from some sort of raffia among many other things. The Arab peddler flung a rope up to the rail of the ship, to which a basket was attached and goods fancied by the passengers were passed up and payment after much haggling lowered down. A Gully- Gully man was allowed aboard and thrilled the children with his conjuring show, causing eggs, chicks and other things to disappear and reappear in most unlikely places.

The ships call here was to be a short one, but allowed time for a brief visit ashore before sailing. In the company of friends I went ashore for a quick look at the town. No doubt there were better parts other than those we visited. What we saw seemed dirty and unattractive and I was not sorry when it was time to return to the ship.

Travelling through the Suez Canal this time was a double pleasure for me, reviving memories of my earlier journeys and enjoying the interest of Jennifer and Virginia in these new sights. The large numbers of troops had gone although some small groups remained in certain areas. Instead we could see the inhabitants of the area going about their normal way of life.

This time being February, we traversed the Red Sea in comfort and without undue incident. The swimming pool was more widely used as the temperature continued to rise. Everyone brought out their summer clothing and colours and health bloomed together.

Our next anchorage was in Colombo and my excitement was every bit as great as that of the children. It was their first opportunity to go ashore since the ship had sailed and they were eager to be on land again. I wondered what changes had taken place in the nine years that had elapsed since I was there. We had only the one-day in which to explore.

Again the vast numbers of service personnel were missing from the town but the sunshine and colour remained. People no longer travelled in rickshaws and the few rickshaws still to be seen in the town centre, appeared to be used for transporting goods. There were far more taxis than I remembered but no beggars on the streets. The ladies making lace had also disappeared. Most of the buildings looked shabbier and in need of some attention and shops and restaurants that had always been busy were empty of customers.

During the nine years I had been away Ceylon had gained its independence and was now known as Sri Lanka, Lanka being the name of the old Sinhalese Kingdom ruled over by the King of Kandy. With the withdrawal of the British Administration and services, had gone much of the wealth and trade on which the country had relied for income. The English language was still widely spoken and we had no difficulty in making ourselves understood. A wander around town and a short taxi trip to take a brief look at Mount Lavinia was all we had time to do before darkness fell. For now we were in tropical zones where there is no twilight and night begins about six thirty p.m.

It had been a nostalgic day for me and a revealing one of the changes that had taken place over the years. The children were tired but excitedly happy with the change of environment, even if only for one day. Back on board they had their evening meal and settled down in their respective bunks. When they awoke next morning Sri Lanka was well behind us and we were that many more miles closer to Singapore and Harry.

Preparations for our arrival in Singapore were hectic. Farewell parties for the children, dinners and dances for the adults, exchanging of addresses with friends made on voyage and of course the packing of all our belongings.

Clock tower and lighthouse, Colombo, Sri Lanka

CHAPTER FOUR
Arrival in Singapore

Tuesday 22.2.55.

As the ship glided onto the final harbour of our passage by sea, the children and I gazed down at the dock searching for Harry among the crowds of people congregating there. The relief and excitement when we saw his face looking upwards searching for us was tremendous. He stood there looking tanned and fit in his tropical shirt and shorts in the strong sunshine. What a contrast it was to the snowy morning in January when we had all said 'goodbye'.

Although back on dry land once more our journey was not yet over. There were still another five hundred miles to go before we reached Penang where we were to make our home for the next three and a half years.

This time we were to travel by train. There were just two trains every twenty- four hours. The day train and the night train. Harry had made bookings for us on the night train where we could get sleeping berths. The time- table showed it would leave Singapore for the journey north at seven pm. That left us with a few hours to talk, we all had plenty to say, and to take in a little of our new surroundings. The RAF dealt with all luggage problems and left us with only personal pieces like Teddy and Virginia's doll, so we were free to look around.

The waterfront was crowded with craft of all kinds from the large liners to Chinese Junks and tiny sampans. The streets were often wide and spacious, the buildings white and Colonial, or Chinese with curved roofs and bright tiles. In the wealthier areas there were many trees and shrubs, imposing gateways and many cars. By contrast the poorer districts had open fronted shops in narrow allies or streets in which tenement buildings housed many families. Poles stretched high above the streets on which the day's washing was hung to dry.

The majority of the population seemed to be Chinese in origin, but occasionally we saw a Hindu Temple crowned with its pyramid cone of carved and highly painted Hindu gods, which denoted the existence of an Indian population also.

In the excitement of our arrival and meeting Harry, everything tended to become a little confused, so we retired to a quieter area to have a cool drink and relax. When it became time to make our way to the train, Harry hailed two trishas. These were a more updated form of rickshaw consisting of a double padded seat with hood, for the passengers, behind which, on a bicycle type seat sat the driver, the whole contraption being mounted on three wheels and peddled by the driver, in this case Chinese. Harry and Jennifer sat in one trishaw and Virginia and me in the other. Harry said "The station" and we set off. Enjoying the slight breeze created as our driver made his way through the traffic. I was able to notice the streets we travelled through and buildings we passed when we came to a quieter area of the town where after a few minutes our drivers stopped. We were about to descend from our trishas when we became aware that the building they had brought us to was not the station we had asked for but the Britannia Club!

The drivers were smiling widely and holding out their hands for their fare. It dawned on us that neither of the drivers spoke English and had not understood a word Harry had said. We did our best to explain that we wanted the station, not the Britannia Club, to no avail. A rather smarter looking Chinese was passing by and Harry enlisted his help. He spoke to our drivers, we thanked him and climbed back into our trishas. Off we went once more, re-passing some of the buildings and streets already travelled and five minutes or so later our drivers stopped again. This time outside the Police Station! " No, no, no," we said, "Not the Police Station, We want the railway station!"

The drivers broke into an incomprehensible gabble of Chinese and soon we had gathered a small crowd of spectators. We appealed to the crowd, but there appeared to be not one person there capable of translating our request to the two drivers. In desperation Harry reverted to mime and did a passable imitation of a steam train, chu-chooing up and down the pavement, arms moving like the wheels of a train.! At last understanding dawned on the faces of drivers and spectators alike. Faces broke into broad smiles, . "Ah! Krayta Api!" they said, and we learnt our first words of Malay for

19

train. There was much chattering and nodding and we were ushered into the trishas once more.

Passing the same streets and buildings for the third time, we at last entered a different area and drew up outside the Railway Station. With only a few minutes to spare, Harry paid off the drivers and we dashed for the train.

By the time the train had travelled from Singapore City to the north of the island, darkness had descended and the children were asleep in their bunk berths. The gently revolving ceiling fan helped to relieve the humidity of the temperature that was well into the 80 degrees. The daytime and night-time temperatures varying very little at that latitude, night temperatures dropped probably only 2 degrees.

Singapore is joined to the mainland of Malaya (now Malaysia) by a long causeway and it is here at the end of the causeway where the train passengers have to submit to an inspection by customs. The customs officers were Malay men, small in stature and neat in appearance. As they came down the corridor checking in every compartment I was concerned that they would wake the children. When they reached our compartment, I put a finger to my lips and quietly slid open the door so that they could see the children sleeping. They were very understanding, smiled and nodded and moved on to the next compartment. This was occupied by a young European male and much to his consternation, the officers showed excessive zeal in searching his compartment. All his belongings were thoroughly checked and spread in the train corridor for inspection before the customs men moved on. The young man was left to gather up and repack everything back into his suitcases. I doubt if he was pleased!

In spite of sensations of excitement and pleasure of reunion, discomfort from the heat of the confined area and apprehension about our new life and home, I did manage some fitful sleep. By early morning the train made its scheduled stop at Kuala Lumper , the main city of Malaya, where we changed for the day train to Penang. Around six p.m. we were chugging in to the station at Prai near Butterworth, an eleven hour journey through jungle and rubber plantations, native villages (Kampongs) and one or two towns.

At Prai we had to transfer from the train on to a ferry to cross the last few miles by sea to the Island of Penang where we planned to live. At that time the ferries were the only connection between the mainland of Malaya and Georgetown, the port town of Penang Island. Now a fine new bridge has been built to take much of the traffic.

The Ferry Terminus was crowded with cars and lorries loaded with produce for the island. The mostly Chinese drivers snatched a quick forty winks while waiting their turn to drive aboard. Other passengers on foot or wheeling bicycles made their way up the gang- planks. The mixture of races was far greater here, five hundred miles up country. Apart from Chinese and Indians there were many more Malay people in their sarong type skirts, the men wearing their black velvet Songkok caps or hats. The women in sarong and kebaya, an attractive blouse- cum-jacket garment. Their heads covered with a light scarf.

The ferry crossing took about twenty minutes. During this time hawkers would offer to sell tins of fruit drinks to the captive and often thirsty passengers. A cabin area provided shelter from sun or rain and a place to sit. As the ferry drew closer to Penang we could see lines of shack like houses of the fishermen built on tall stilts and stretching like tentacles into the sea. On our right and behind the ferry landing area were docks and warehouses, known as go-downs, of the port. The dock itself was full of tongkangs, wooden sailing vessels many of them with a painted eye on the prow to ward off evil spirits. These carried cargoes of rubber, copra, betalnuts and other goods to and from ports around Malaysia and down to Singapore.

If you should arrive at low tide, probably the first notable thing would be the smell. It was strong and penetrating and definitely not the best type of toilet water! In time one could become inured to it and manage to pass through without reaching for your handkerchief or even wrinkling your nose.

Penang being a free port, there were no custom formalities required of us here. Although passengers boarding the ferry for the mainland would need to go through the usual customs checks, in this case usually carried out by the tall bearded and turbaned Sikhs.

The very last stage of our journey was made by taxi to the Hotel Metropole in Northam Road where we were to stay until we were able to find our own living accommodation.

Ferry to Penang from Prai near Butterworth

Singapore River and Cavanagh Bridge

A Hindu Temple, Singapore

The Johore Causeway, Singapore

Penang Waterfront

Penange Waterfront, Georgetown from the sea

CHAPTER FIVE

Introduction to Penang

The six weeks we spent in the Hotel Metropole gave us time to adjust to our new country. We began to recognize the people of varying nationalities around us and to distinguish their roles in the community. Most commercial life seemed to be carried out by the Chinese and Indian population. The Malay people being more prominent in the regions of government and security services such as the Police Force that appeared to be almost entirely composed of Malays with European Officers.

The hotel manager was a tall Eurasian, friendly and helpful towards his guests. His staff was mostly Chinese and it was from our stay here that the whole family developed a taste for Chinese style cuisine. A little later when we had a Malay amah (servant) we enlarged our palate to include Malay curries.

Other guests at the hotel among the Europeans there were families of RAF personnel recently arrived and waiting for accommodation in quarters at Butterworth, the Air Force Station on the mainland. There were Police Officers on leave from up country, Planters for a weekend break and business men from Singapore, or one of the other towns sited at intervals on the long west coast of Malaya. When the race meeting season was in full swing a number of Australian Jockeys would use the hotel as their base.

The rooms were large with high ceilings from which the much-needed fan revolved. Some of the rooms were shaded by verandahs in the old Colonial style. Each bedroom had its own shower room. This consisted of a smaller room with tiled floor, a water pipe running down one wall from the ceiling to about 3ft from the floor. Beneath this stood a large terracotta bowl and a smaller one that was used to douse oneself with the water. This was all a great novelty to our daughters who needed no persuasion to use it.

After only two weeks in Penang, much to our surprise Virginia developed measles and she and I were confined to our room until all signs of spots had disappeared. Luckily it was not a bad case and she was not unduly affected but we did not wish to risk passing it on. I had told the hotel manager and we were able to move to one of the small chalets in the grounds of the hotel. Virginia had probably caught the infection from a child on the ship.

Harry had arranged for Jennifer (aged 7) to start at the local British Army School. As it was only a few yards further down on the same road it presented no difficulty. We still had no transport of our own and had to rely on trishas and taxis to make trips into town for shopping or visits to the beach or swimming club. As many of the drivers spoke no English, I found it useful to learn a few words of Malay in order to make myself understood. There are two forms of Malay language, Pure Malay being a complicated form of polite language. I bought a book on the more simple Bazaar Malay that I hoped would be sufficient for my needs.

Virginia had her fourth birthday while we were still in the hotel. Hotel life is constricting for a small child and although I had done my best to keep her occupied with various games and forms of handcraft work, we were restricted for space and movement. Now that she had turned four she was entitled to join the nursery group attached to the Army School her sister attended. Here she would have companions and more interests.

Unfortunately Virginia did not see it in quite this way and yelled very loudly every time I left her for every morning of the first week. I was reassured by the teacher in charge, telling me that the yelling stopped as soon as I was out of sight and Virginia then settled down quite happily to play with the other children. Jennifer presented no such problem and had joined in the school routine without any trouble.

Gradually we were getting to know other European expatriates whose wives were helpful in initiating me into the ways of domestic life in a hot climate. I was escorted into town and guided to the best shopping areas and restaurants or hotels where one could cool off with an iced tea or coffee. The Cold Storage Creameries ice cream parlour was a favoured place for the family. Not only did they serve delicious milk shakes, but also it was one of the few buildings to be air-conditioned.

The only other buildings to be air conditioned at that time were the cinemas. There, the contrast in temperature with that outside was so great that it was necessary to take a cardigan or stole to keep from shivering.

After six weeks we were able to move temporarily from the hotel, into a large Chinese House whose owner was going to Europe on a five month visit. The house was built in typical Malayan Chinese style and fronted by a white wall. Pillars supporting metal gates opened onto a semi circular driveway to the main door of the house which continued past the kitchen quarters to a second pair of pillars and gates, leading back to the road.

In the garden a Frangipani tree scented the air with its exotic fragrance. Shrubs and plants decorated the borders but most of the rest of the garden was laid as lawn. A gardener was employed by the Chinese owner to maintain the garden in good order and we agreed to keep him on part-time enabling us to enjoy the benefits of his work.

In a letter home I described the garden this way " the vegetation is very lush….We get plenty of rain so everything is very green all the year. In the garden are Chrysanthemums, Petunias, daisy types, Zinnias and pinks. We also have Papaya trees, their fruit is very much like the Paw Paw you get canned. There are other plants of beautiful colours and many Orchids, but I have yet to learn their names."

Inside the house the rooms were large and airy with high ceilings from which the essential fans were suspended. Many windows having shutters to keep out the hot sun. The shutters mostly made of wooden slats, but some having coloured glass inserts. The doors of the house were of the double variety and had to be bolted and barred at night as burglary was rife in the town.

Downstairs all the floors were tiled, but upstairs they were painted and polished to a high gloss that responded to a mop or damp cloth for cleaning. There were four bedrooms one contained a traditional, carved, wooden Chinese bed. To us it looked hard and most uninviting. Luckily all other beds were of western taste and very comfortable.

The girls were delighted with their bedroom which boasted a small balcony overlooking the single story roof of the kitchen quarters. We were unaware that allocating the girls this room was to cause us a near heart attack later on.

Virginia at four was an adventurous youngster, always looking for a new challenge. The roof below her balcony gave her the opportunity for new ventures. Her father and I were sitting in the garden one day chatting to friends, when I looked up to see our four year old daughter doing a tight rope act along the ridge of the kitchen roof. Concentrating fiercely, with arms outstretched she balanced her way along the narrow ridge to the end of the roof, about fifteen feet to twenty feet in length, carefully turned and retraced her way the same distance back again to the balcony where she nonchalantly climbed back into her bedroom.

All this time, we in the garden below could do nothing but hold our breath, for had we called out she would probably have been startled and fallen. Once she was safely inside we dashed up the stairs and father read out the riot act!

Other rooms in the house included four bathrooms, two upstairs and two downstairs none of which had long baths, but instead large upright tubs under taps, similar in style to those in the hotel, except that in the house they were tiled and cube shaped. A sitting room, two dining rooms and study occupied the main space downstairs and of course there was the kitchen and servants quarters as an annex to the main building.

The dining area was a long L shaped area off the main stairs which held two elongated tables around one of which were placed eighteen chairs, tall, wooden and hard seated. Looking down on this vast table were many portraits of Chinese who we presumed to be members of the owner's family. All were somewhat forbidding as though afraid to smile.

I admit to finding them rather intimidating!

The study housed a huge desk with which Harry was delighted and planned to do much of his work there. Furnishings in the sitting room were something of a shock. Armchairs were of wood, unyielding and painted bright blue, as were tables and sideboards. All tables except those in the dining room, had glass tops as did the sideboards so they were easy to keep clean, a useful consideration when young children are around.

The kitchen was my biggest bugbear. Walking in from the sunlight, the kitchen seemed large, dark, and long but cool. When my eyes became accustomed to the darkness I was taken aback to find a large brick island in the middle of the tiled floor. It puzzled me until I looked closer and discovered it enclosed the position of a charcoal fire. The only means provided for cooking meals. The Chinese version of the Victorian cooking range.

Since I had only cooked by gas or electricity before, never on a range or even an AGA, this was going to be a bit of a problem. Still, the family had to be fed and we had not yet had time to find servants. It was over two months since I had had to make a meal myself and I felt very much out of practice. A simple meal it would have to be for our first day. Metaphorically rolling up the sleeves of my sleeveless dress, I went into battle.

Using some newspaper on which I balanced two or three pieces of charcoal, I attempted to build a fire within the stove. The newspaper burned but the charcoal did not. I tried again. After several attempts I saw a spark. Fanning furiously and spluttering from the smoke aroused, I finally produced a fire. Before it had time to die again, I whipped my frying pan over, flung in some sausages and kept fanning. After a couple of hours, red eyed, tousle-haired, smutty faced but triumphant, I carried plates of sausages and eggs to my hungry family.

Neither the family, nor I, was eager to have a repeat performance of this occasion and so a new stove and a cook were priorities on our shopping list. A stove was comparatively easy, the cook was not. Since we could find no suitable electric points and gas was not available, we resorted to a paraffin stove with an oven. Again, it was a venture into the unknown for me. Once I had it lit; the various dials were easy enough to cope with, although the smell took some getting used to. At least I was able to produce some decent meals.

A young Indian had presented himself at our door saying he was a cook. As I was desperate, I agreed to give him a try. At this time we had one amah, Anno, working for us who cleaned the house and did the washing. With Anno as interpreter, I took on the young man for a trial period.

On his first day, in order to make things easy for him I bought the ingredients and asked him to prepare a salad. At the agreed lunch hour, the girls, Harry and I sat at the dining table and waited.

Our cook came in and presented us with his efforts. A dish of boiled lettuce, fried beetroot, and whole potatoes, rock hard. There were one or two other items all equally uneatable. I spent four days trying to teach him some European cooking before we parted by mutual consent.

Valli who replaced the young man was also Indian. She too was young, in her twenties, had worked for Europeans before and was a good cook. She had a pleasant personality and was approved of by all the family. She also spoke reasonable English that made life easier for me.

With the household problems off my mind and the children at school each morning, I had time on my hands. A Red Cross group was active in Georgetown and I was persuaded to join. The members were mostly ladies from the European section of the community with a few Chinese ladies from the local population. Our interests included the outlying islands where there was a tuberculosis sanatorium and also a leper colony. On the main island there was the big Penang hospital. There were also other activities such as fund raising to keep us all occupied.

After a few visits, the organizer asked me if I would go with her to Penang hospital where she had discovered there was a small ward of boys attached to the men's ward. The boys, some, but not all bed bound were enclosed in a long narrow ward without windows and with no interests to occupy them during the day. The nurses complained that they were very naughty and caused a lot of trouble. "Could I do anything for them?" I was asked. All the boys were Chinese and non- English speaking. My few words of Malay would not get me far. However it seemed a worthwhile challenge, so I agreed to have a go.

My first problem was communication. Since I knew no Chinese I must teach them English. I found their names unpronounceable and impossible to remember all at once, therefore they would all have English nicknames. These I wrote in large letters on cards that I pinned over each bed, JOHN, JOE, TOM, DICK, BOB etc. The names were greeted with great delight and hilarity and some time was spent in learning each other's new name. Later I discovered that even the nurses joined in the fun and used the English names.

The Red Cross allowed me small funds with which to buy pencils, crayons, paper and games. Pictures of various parts of the body were cut out of magazines and pasted onto a chart and identified, such as hand, head, leg, foot, and face. I did similar charts for clothes, articles, animals and anything else I could think of. These were pinned around the ward so that the boys could amuse themselves by testing each other when I was not with them. As the staff did not remove the charts I can only assume that Matron did not disapprove.

29

In the time I spent with the children each week, we practiced speaking English, drew pictures and played games together. After a few weeks we were joined by an Indian girl of about nine years of age with a badly burned back, who was brought in by one of the Sisters to share in the fun. We named her Mary.

It was a very rewarding experience especially when I was told how much the children's behaviour had improved.

As a healthy young woman I was not naturally motivated towards hospitals and sickbeds and had never been in the slightest way inclined towards any form of nursing. In truth I had had to steel myself to enter the hospital and some of the sights and smells appalled me, but the welcome smiles and interest given by the children made it all worth while.

Hotel Metropole, Penang

9 Clove Hall Road

British Army School

CHAPTER SIX
Meeting the People

Living in the Chinese House brought us into closer contact with the local life. Every day hawkers would pass our house uttering their strange calls. Some on bicycles, some pushing barrows others carrying their small stalls on a bamboo cane balanced over their shoulder. They sold all manner of goods from live chickens to curry and lemonade. The hardware man had his tricycle so laden with pots, pans, brushes and cans, that it was a wonder he could see his way. Children flocked to the man who sold the flavoured balls of ice, but who would want to buy from the mobile butcher whose slabs of raw meat hung from a rail before him on his tricycle, open to all the dust, flies and heat of the roads he travelled?. Certainly not me!

Across the road from us lived a Malay family and Jennifer and Virginia made friends with their young daughter Bebe, who often came to play in the garden. Bebe introduced us to the Rambutan fruit, a red fleshy, sweet tasting small fruit encased in a prickly green case resembling that of a horse chestnut and like the horse chestnut grown on spreading shady trees. Bebe's family had some of these trees growing in their garden. Once recognised, we noticed large baskets of Rambutans for sale at points along the roadside during our travels. Often offered for sale at the same time were other fruits in prickly green cases. These were Durians, much larger, about the size of a melon. It was impossible not to notice a Durian; its smell was so strong and so vile. It has been described as a mixture between bad drains and onions and is so overpowering that it penetrated everything. We were told that if you could ignore the smell the taste was delicious. I never got close enough to find out. It was too difficult to eat whilst holding your nose!

Life in our new home was interesting though not exactly peaceful. On one side of us was a building used as a weight lifting club. When the weights were dropped our whole house vibrated and I feared for the crockery that rattled alarmingly.

On the other side was another building housing a Mah Jong school. This was quiet enough during the day, but became active every evening when we would hear the click, click of the Mah Jong tiles in constant use. The clicking noise would continue into the small hours of the morning. Sometimes it was five am before the players gave up and went home.

When after four months the opportunity came to move to a small flat, we were overjoyed. A block of six flats had been erected in European style by a Chinese Towkey (landlord) who wished to rent them to Europeans, mainly because they had fewer children than the Chinese, but also because he could ask for higher rents. The flats were still within easy reach of the Army School and would also be convenient for my husband's work and the new job I was taking up as a teacher in a private school.

Before making the move we took the family for a week's holiday in the Cameron Highlands, about one hundred miles journey from Penang and around four to five thousand feet above sea level. A breath of fresh hill air would do us all a world of good. As yet we had no transport of our own, so started our journey by taking the train to Ipoh. Here we found a taxi driver willing to make the journey into the hills.

At this time, 1954, the Communist Terrorists, or C.Ts as they were referred to, were still very active in many parts of Malaya. The country was divided into White Areas and Black Areas. The White Areas were parts of the country supposedly free of terrorist activity and therefore comparatively safe to travel through. The Black Areas were those where there were known to be bands of C.Ts roaming and where you were likely to be in danger of attack.

The Cameron Highlands and roads leading to it were all in a designated Black area. If you were travelling in such an area you were advised to wait for a police or army escort. Harry and I considered the prospect carefully and came to the conclusion that as we had noticed the police and army vehicles were the prime targets for attacks, we would probably be safer travelling solo, without escort. The taxi driver was agreeable and we set off.

Once away from Ipoh the road began to climb. We soon left the flatter coastal region and followed the twists and turns upwards through roads enclosed by thick jungle. As we climbed the road became more narrow and the bends sharper. It was at this point that our taxi caught up with a slow moving lorry piled high with Durian fruit. Because of the narrow road and continual bends it was impossible to pass and we had to spend the next fifty miles crawling behind the truck and choking with the overpowering stench emanating from the Durians. Great was our relief on arrival at the hill resort as we turned off to the track leading to the Smoke House Inn and left the lorry to go its own way.

Although the fringes of the resort were still edged by jungle even here, four thousand feet up, the air was cool and free of the cloying heat experienced on the coastal plains. In spite of the trying journey we all began to perk up and looked forward to the next few days.

The Smoke House Inn was built in the style of an old English home, complete with oak beams. The manager was an Indian, that somehow seemed out of keeping as everything else was obviously so English orientated. However, he was charming and made us all very comfortable.

The surrounding garden matched the house in its old English style even to the sundial set in a paved area among rose beds. At this altitude flowers that would stand no chance of blooming on the coastal regions could thrive here. Close by the hotel were several little streams of clear water, a pleasant change from the usual mud clouded water of the rivers nearer the coast. On their banks grew wild Montbretia, its tall stems of orange flowers adding a splash of welcome colour to the general and often monotonous green of the surrounding jungle. On other banks wild orchids grew and strange cup like flowers holding liquid whose local name was Monkey Pitchers.

A change from exploring the local walks was provided by the golf course situated only a few yards from the hotel. Here I played my one and only game of golf. The golf course was intersected by those delightful streams of water, outcrops of jungle and minor chasms. It took me hours to hit my way around it and I have never counted up to ten under my breath so often before or since!

We all slept well through the cool nights under our blankets and by the end of the week were refreshed and ready to face the move into our new flat.

Our journey home was by taxi all the way from Smoke House Inn to Penang stopping for lunch at Ipoh and tea at Taiping where we strolled in the town's attractive park. We had no problem with the CTs who were known to be around, but like other road travelers, we were obliged to stop at the frequent road checkpoints. Here, searches were made by the army and police to ensure that no one carried arms or food that could be passed to or taken by the CTs.

However on twenty- first of November 1955 about a week after our return, we heard on the news that a large- scale raid by a hundred CTs had been carried out on Keay Farm. An area only a few miles away from where we had stayed, and much damage was done. We were lucky!

Stall Holder

Seller of ice balls

The Hardware Man

Smoke House Inn

Gardens of Smoke House Inn, Cameron Highlands

Mobile Stall Trader, Penang

CHAPTER SEVEN

Our Second Home in Penang

Our move into the new flat was delayed another week which gave us time to order furniture and equipment. Shopping in town was an interesting and time-consuming activity. Those shops of the same trade were usually grouped together in the same street. For instance, one would find half a dozen tinsmiths and an equal number of shops selling hardware goods all next to one another on one side of a street and on the other side might be several shoe shops where they not only sold but made foot ware to a customer's specification.

We did not walk into these open fronted shops and expect to find the goods priced for us to see. That would be no fun for the shopkeeper. It was necessary to ask the price of each item in which one was interested and then to haggle until you had at least halved the first asking price.

In the street of furniture makers it was fascinating to watch them making the bamboo or rattan furniture. To bend the cane to the required shape, a man would squat before a charcoal fire set on the floor in the middle of the shop. Over this fire he warmed a length of cane gradually bending it as it became more flexible. Then when the correct shape was obtained, he tied it taut with string before leaving it to cool and continue with the next piece. Our dining room table, dining chairs and three- piece suite were all made in this way. The Dunlopillo cushions needed to be ordered from another small shop and the material to make the covers came from yet another store.

The set of small glass topped tables caused more discussion and haggling. We considered the carving on much of the Chinese furniture vastly overdone and requested a set of four small tables in light coloured teakwood with just a small amount of carving. To our surprise we were charged a higher price. "Why is the price higher, when there is less carving?" we asked. "Only little carving, so must use much better wood. " Was the answer. We gave in.

In due course, we and the furniture were installed in the new flat on the top floor of a group of six apartments. The accommodation consisted of a large living room, two bedrooms, and a bathroom with long western style bath. This was a real luxury to us, although the Malay people frowned upon its use, likening we Europeans to the water buffalo that enjoys lying in muddy pools. The Malay people were required as Muslims to wash their bodies beneath running water three times daily.

There was also a modern tiled kitchen fitted with work and cupboard units and a bedroom shower and toilet for an amah complete with small balcony. The flat was small enough to require one amah only, and so we took Valli who agreed to cook and clean for us. Valli's husband also came with her and as we were not on a bus route, we provided them with the money to buy a bicycle to enable him to get to work.

The children were collected by army transport complete with armed guard, to go to school each day, as strange as it seemed, Penang was still considered to be a Black Area at that time. Harry, my husband was taken by RAF Transport from the Island to the mainland each day and I arranged for a trisha to convey me to my place of work. I had discovered that with the use of only a few words of Malay, poosing kanan, (turn right), poosing keeree, (turn left), nantee (wait), brentee (stop) and roomah (house), I could make myself understood and get around quite well.

The school in which I taught was housed in the premises of the local Masonic Lodge. The building was known to the local population as Roomah Huntu,(House of Ghosts). It seemed that all Masonic Lodges were so named, although I never discovered why this should be so.

Shortly after our move we were in a position to be able to afford to invest in a car. After the usual bargaining process with the Chinese owner of a garage, Harry arrived home driving a bright blue Wolsey 680 car. The price paid was reasonable we discovered because the car had been involved in an accident in which someone had died and the superstitious local population would not touch it. Death loomed large in the minds of the Chinese people of Malaya. We were told that many old people who were close to death would crawl outside to await their end, rather than die in the house.

The large boat shaped coffins we saw being made were often carved with various symbols or designs and a Chinese funeral was an elaborate procession involving a decorated hearse, Professional Mourners covered in white with streaked faces and uttering wailing cries. Two or three bands of musicians, depending on how wealthy the family were, also accompanied the procession and played any tune they could manage. Western music was popular with the bands and many of the tunes were quite incongruous and seemingly to be completely out of keeping for a funeral.

It was surprising there were not more funerals, due to the habit of some young Chinese, who would wait until the very last moment to cross the road in front of cars. Believing this way, that by a near miss from death, the devil would be cut from their tails or heels.

The car made a tremendous difference to our lives, enabling us to explore other parts of the island and take the children to the beaches more often. To make more use of the car it was sensible that I should learn to drive, so I duly enrolled for lessons with a Chinese instructor. His attitude to users of the road was interesting. On one occasion at a roundabout when another driver had failed to obey the highway code and had pulled out in front of me, my instructor became very annoyed and excited "Hit him, hit him" he cried. "But what about your car? " I said "Am insured" he replied "Hit him"!

Luckily by the time we had exchanged these pleasantries the other car was out of reach of any action on my part!

On another tuition period, I was driving along when he told me to stop. I put my foot on the brake, but the car continued on. "Stop, stop" he said. "Use the brake". "I am using the brake," I said, pressing as hard as I could. It was no use; the brakes failed to work. As luck had it we were on a quiet road with little traffic and by using the hand brake we came to no harm. It was not the case with a friend of ours who was also learning to drive with the same instructor. She had gone into a brick wall and returned home with a broken arm.

Other hazards to driving were the large monsoon drains that lined every road in town. These were necessary to take the flow of excessive rainwater in the monsoon season. There were times when we visited the cinema on a normal hot, but dry evening and at the end of the film, left the cinema having to wade through water filled streets to reach our car. In the short time we had been watching the film the rain had been so heavy it had overflowed the deep drains and spread like a river through the town. Then you needed to watch your step carefully to avoid a sudden plunge and unpleasant wetting, in these hidden gullies. It was a frequent sight to see cars stuck halfway in a monsoon drain.

Several months after moving into our flat, Valli left us to have a baby and Zainab (pronounced Zenna) took her place. Zenna was Malay and spoke little English, but was pleasant, helpful and willing to learn. To communicate, I had to practice my Malay, learning new words to explain menus and methods. I believe that Zenna's English improved more rapidly than did my Malay, and our language problems had surprising results at times, as when I asked for mushrooms and got sausages, but nothing disastrous occurred and eventually we understood one another very well.

Zenna was barefooted in the flat, but we always knew when she was around as we would hear her many bracelets jingling as she moved. The Malay women wore their wealth in Jewellery. When they had a little money it would be invested in a new gold bracelet or necklace. Wearing their wealth could be hazardous with so many thieves about and Zenna had a necklace snatched from her neck while she was cycling home one day.

Zenna had asked permission to sleep in her own home each night. The reason she gave was that her thatched attap house was so much cooler than the modern flats. Her house stood in a small kampong or village a little way outside town on the main coast road. Built on stilts three to four feet off the ground it consisted of one largish room and two smaller rooms. There was very little furniture. Apart from one table I have no recollection of anything else in the large room. Mats made of palm leaves took the place of beds. Certainly it would be cooler as the thatched roof sloped to form a shady veranda and the woven walls and roughly shaped planks of the wooden floor so far above the ground allowed what breeze there was to flow through the whole house.

The village was kept clean and the children seemed healthy and happy, sharing their village playground among the houses with a number of chickens. Trees, including coconut palms that provided food and drink shaded the whole kampong. A standpipe provided good clean water.

On the evenings we required Zenna to stay for 'baby sitting' purposes. She would sleep in the amah's quarters in the flat.

Thieves were a problem to everyone and precautions had to be taken. Because of the close humidity of the climate, even at night, it was tempting to leave your doors and windows open to take advantage of every little breath of air, but to be safe it was necessary to make sure all doors and balcony windows were securely fastened. Our modern flats had louvre windows that we left slightly ajar. Even these were no proof against thieves who devised a tool consisting of a hook on the end of a long bamboo pole, the length of which was implanted with sharp razor blades. With this implement thieves could hook rings, watches and other pieces of jewellery from tops of dressing tables etc. Should you wake and try to grab the pole, the razorblades would cut your hands severely.

The wealthier Chinese all had barred or wrought iron windows or shutters and frequently kept large fierce dogs who roamed the grounds at night.

Even by day, thieves were audacious. A friend of ours went to a beach out of town to swim. While he was in the water a thief came and stole his clothes. He was left high and not so dry in only his swimming trunks in which to return to town.! An embarrassing situation! Other friends, also spending a day on the coast returned to their carefully locked, parked car, to find it minus four wheels!

Street Scene Penang

Street Scene Penang

Street Scene Penang

Looking down from our flat on Kalawi Road

Kalawi Road

Masonic Lodge, "Roomah Huntu" Western Road School

The children were delighted with our bright blue car

Street scene, Penang

Penang Market

Malayan Railway Building, Penang

CHAPTER EIGHT
Festivals

Much of the fascination of living in a country peopled by so many different races is the interest provided by the varied customs, foods, and festivals of culture and religion. Everyone took advantage of the many holidays provided by the religious or national festivals and it took some calculating and consultation of the calendar to discover on which days the banks would be open!

Not far from our new home was a large Hindu temple, The Nattakkottai Chettiar Temple in Waterfall Road. This was the focus of a big celebration each year when pilgrims came to ask the favour of, or do penance to the Gods. The three-day festival was called Thai Pusam and took place in February, marking the victory of the Lord Subramaniam over a demon that was inclined to transfer mountains. The procession was a rather gruesome sight for the sensitive. Many of those taking part had cheeks or tongues impaled by long sharp needles or spikes, others had hooks fixed into the skin on their backs from which strong threads of twine were attached. These in turn were tied to a small cart that was dragged along behind the pilgrim, literally by the skin of their back. Others had numerous fine spears stuck into back and chest that supported a decorated semi-circular frame around their body and over the head. These were known as Kavahdi.

Each of these penitents had his or her small group of supporters who carried a small stool with them to enable the pilgrim to take an occasional rest during the long five miles of the course to the temple. There was never any sign of blood on any of the participants and all appeared to be in some sort of trance as they gyrated their way along to the chanting and encouragement of their friends and families.

On reaching the temple they were guided inside where priests removed the hooks, spears, and spikes and smeared a white paste over their bodies. When they left the temple, apart from the white paste effect, they appeared completely normal and free of any signs of pain or the trance-like state in which they were held only a short time before.

The festival also had its pleasurable side for those not so intimately involved. Stalls, side shows, boat swings and other amusements of which the young took advantage, were installed in an area near the temple. The climax of the religious celebration that took place at this same temple was when the image of Lord Subramaniam was taken from the Chettia Temple and returned to its temple in the town.

The gilded statue sparkling with jewels was set high in a canopied, richly decorated silver chariot drawn by white bulls, pushed by women in fulfilment of vows, all escorted by white robed priests. The chariot was preceded by two or three bands of musicians, usually one group of traditional Indian Nageaswara instrumentalists and other musicians of Chinese race, dressed in tatty kahki shorts, singlets and shirts, playing western style tunes, their playing frequently matching their dress. These players were outflanked by hired Chinese men carrying tall lamps. The bedecked and tasselled bullocks made their slow progress along the road, followed by more Indian musical parties who sang holy songs of Lord Subramaniam. As they moved along Hindu believers smashed coconuts on the road in front of the bullocks and mothers rolled their small babies in their path hoping in this way to gain the blessings and protection of the god for their children.

Small trays holding a broken coconut and flaming coconut oil were handed up by worshipers to the priest who offered them to the god. The trays were then handed back and the recipient, dipping his finger into a substance on the tray, made a yellow spot in the centre of his or her forehead and salaamed to the statue. Thousands of coconuts were broken open and the milk allowed to seep into a stream in which young men bathed in order to purify themselves. The kernels of the nuts were eaten to ensure good health. During this festival time, no Hindu was allowed to lend money.

Chinese New Year is celebrated on the first full moon of the New Year, by the big Chingay Procession. The most notable parts of this festival were the huge gaily coloured, silk flags carried by the various groups of men. The Groups were formed from different trades such as the fish workers, tinsmiths, or other market traders.

Fixed to bamboo poles twenty feet or more in height, they were not simply carried, but were juggled by men who balanced these huge waving flag poles on shoulders, necks, elbows and even chins, adroitly changing from one position to another with a twist of the body.

Many car bonnets and roofs suffered severe denting in the weeks preceding the festival, while the young men practised their skills.

Apart from the flag wavers, decorated floats with costumed passengers on well-disguised lorries, trishas, and carts added bright interest as well as colour to the procession. Troops of men in unusual soldier outfits with helmets, shining spears and swords marched in formation before their flags and floats. Each group accompanied by its own musicians on drums and cymbals. Combined with the shouts of spectators and participants, the noise was deafening!

Of all the participants in the Chingay our children were most fascinated by the Chinese Lion, as it pranced along the street, shaking its shaggy mane and rolling its ball-like eyes to scare the onlookers as it made mock attacks towards them and the female figure before it. The female figure was a man dressed in woman's clothes, wearing a white mask and carrying a fan that he fluttered in a feminine fashion.

Another favourite was the dragon whose long gaudy body was supported by the heads and arms of a team of men who twined and twisted their way along through the crowds lining the path of the procession.

On such an occasion traffic in the town came to a virtual standstill until the procession dispersed. Since the whole parade took at least one hour to pass us, there were many frustrated drivers, but generally the festival was a good humoured, lively and happy occasion.

One year proved an exception. The festival was usually paraded for two days. Harry and I decided to take the children into town to see it on its first day. We had an excellent view and joined the crowds in their happy excitement.

Our neighbours chose to go on the second day and arrived in town to find frightened people fleeing in all directions. It appeared that in one section of the procession, excitement had got out of control. A riot had broken out between some Chinese and Malays and people had been stabbed. The result was that the whole town was put under curfew between the hours of five p.m. and five am for a week.

Everyone was included in the curfew and for that week the town population was unsettled and apprehensive. There were further incidents of stabbing and police patrols were much in evidence. Altogether 6 men were killed and 76 people injured, no Europeans were involved. Confined to our flats every evening we whiled away our time reading, listening to music and playing Scrabble with our neighbours. By the end of the week the situation had calmed down and the curfew was lifted. For a while people walked warily, but it was not long before all was back to normal although out bursts like this occurred periodically throughout the Federation of Malaya when tempers were roused.

One such riot broke out in Singapore and caused the Duke of Edinburgh's planned visit to be diverted to Penang. Penang was not prepared for such an honour and no decorations were at hand. It seemed that the same decorations were passed around for formal celebrations from State to State and at this time they were in some other place. Instead the Chingay flags were pressed into service, groups of them being strategically placed on every roundabout along the route the Duke would drive. Unfortunately it rained during the night and all the colours ran, causing them to resemble streaky rainbows. Although I am sure it would not have bothered our distinguished visitor.

At the end of the visit, we took the children to watch the Duke leave by helicopter from the Padang, a large open grassy area, near the hospital and take flight for his next destination.

A story we heard regarding the Duke's visit concerned his arrival in Kuala Lumpur. There was a heavy rainstorm whilst the officials were assembled and awaiting the plane's landing at Kuala Lumpur Airport. The sun had reappeared by the time the Duke emerged from the aircraft. Tenku Abdul Rahman, the Prime Minister of Malaya greeted his Royal Highness and escorted him to the awaiting official open topped car. The Duke seated himself, then arose hurriedly. The back seat was a pool of water. Unfortunately, nobody had remembered to put up the hood of the car when it rained! The Tenku had sat with the Duke at the same time. He remained seated. The Duke looked at him and said, "If you can do it, I suppose I can too"!

The big Malay festival was Hari Raya Puasa. The day of

celebration at the end of the month long fast of Ramadan when the Chief Muslim Priest, the Kathi gave the sign of the end of the fast at the appearance of the new moon. The Muslims were at liberty to eat during the hours of daylight once again, so food played a large part in the celebrations. Our amah was given a holiday on this day, but on one occasion returned to bring us a taste of their festive foods, among them some dainty triangular wafer biscuits and some very strongly flavoured solid jellies called Agga Agga. The biscuits were popular with the children, but they were not so keen on the jellies that were so highly scented.

It was a lovely sight to see the attractive Malay women dressed in their finery and pretty sarongs, kebaya and flimsy headscarves, gathered together like a flock of brightly plumed birds. The men would wear sarongs woven with gold and silver thread; these sarongs were carefully saved and only appeared on such special days.

Celebrations would include a gathering of stalls, side-shows and amusements and most likely a shadow puppet play in which cut out and leather-jointed puppets on long rods were manipulated behind a screen placed in front of a bright light. The puppeteer worked his characters so that their inflated shadows were cast onto the screen, before which sat the audience. The stories were generally traditional, well known and loved by many of the audience.

Christmas was celebrated by the European and Christian members of the population with the traditional church services and carols, although it was a little ironic singing about the "Bleak Mid Winter" when at Christmas we were approaching our hottest period of the year! It took a little ingenuity to explain Father Christmas's method of arrival when we had no chimneys for him to climb down, and artificial snow and Christmas trees and holly somehow lacked the authenticity of the real thing. But the Hong Kong made decorations were delightfully festive and much appreciated by the children.

In spite of the heat, everyone enjoyed the traditional fare and wives were expected to provide the usual mince pies and Christmas puddings. Since such items were not usually available and had to be specially imported it was necessary to start preparations very early and be on hand when they arrived at the stores. The shopkeepers of all nationalities joined in the Christmas Spirit and presented their customers with gifts. Our Indian grocer sent a mixed parcel of goodies, including sweets and hairbrushes for the children and our Chinese greengrocer sent a basket of fruit.

A colleague of mine returned home one day to be told by her amah that the butcher had sent her a turkey. "That's nice. Where is it?" she asked. "In the bathroom Mem" replied her amah. "The bathroom?!" exclaimed Mem. Puzzled she opened the bathroom door to be confronted by a large turkey, very much alive and strutting up and down the bathroom floor. I can't remember the outcome of this particular story, except that it did not remain long in the bathroom!

One year Father Christmas arrived at Butterworth RAF Station in a train made from bomb trolleys. He was greeted by the Station Master (Harry) dressed in top hat and frock coat. Dressed in his long red robe and hood with his long white whiskers, Father Christmas valiantly withstood the blazingly hot sun while he distributed presents to all the assembled children. The children were given a marvellous time at Christmas with parties and presents and if it all became a little too exciting parents could take them for a quiet day on the beach to restore normality.

My young hospital patients were not forgotten at these times and Harry and I visited them taking small gifts to enable them to share the spirit of Christmas with us.

At Chinese New Year and other festivals, Chinese people presented each other with 'Ang Pow' or small gifts, wrapped in red paper as red is the colour denoting happiness and good luck. At the festival of the eighth moon in September, the gifts consisted of small cakes.

In June 1956, Penang held a two-day Water Festival. Stands were built on the shore along Gurney Drive, their strong cotton coverings providing shade and protection from the brilliant sun for the spectators. The events took place each afternoon over the two days and included swimming, sailing, rowing and obstacle races.

Jousting from sampans was an event much enjoyed by the spectators as invariably one or both contestants ended up falling in the sea, but since a wetting in that climate was a positive pleasure, nobody objected.

Prahus, small local vessels that may be rowed or paddled were raced with great enthusiasm. The nine paddle prahus with their leaders standing in the prows exhorting the paddlers with their cries, caused great excitement among the onlookers spurring on their chosen crews with shouts of encouragement.

Water tug of war with teams of eight men standing in four foot of water, pillow fights on a bar over the same depth of water were fun to all as was the challenge of climbing the greasy pole. Skill was called into play for the water ski exhibition, a relatively new sport in 1956 and great skill was also displayed by the pilot and crew of the large helicopter that hovered, turned and almost seemed to complete somersaults over our fascinated heads.

The greatest excitement of the festivities was the race of the Dragon Boats. On the 5th day of the 5th Moon is the traditional day for the Dragon Boat Race. These long shallow boats painted and decorated with their dragon heads and tails, contained crews of twenty two or so paddlers along with a steersman standing with his long pole at the dragons tail. Another member stood in the prow at the dragons head with a small cloth or flag shouting the strokes and a drummer and cymbal player emphasised the strokes by striking on their instruments.

With seven boats taking part, each cheered on by the supporters of the crew's clans, the noise generated must have echoed across the sea all the way to the mainland. Great was the jubilation among their well- wishers when the boat of the Chew Clan came first at the finishing post.

The Water Festival ended with a spectacular pageant of illuminated floats, gently moving past the spectators on the shore, to the accompaniment of soothing music from the musicians aboard. The coloured lights reflecting on the dark water vying with the starlit sky was all in tranquil contrast to the earlier excitements.

A replica of the Taj Mahal aglow with soft lighting was entered by the members of the Indian community among floats from other groups and of course the Dragon Boats were there highly decorated with thousands of coloured bulbs resembling fiery sea serpents as they benignly glided by. Fifty different vessels were displayed before the crowds lining the shore until the festival was brought to its grand final by a lavish fireworks display provided by the U.S. Navy who sent myriads of coloured stars to burst in the sky by man's earlier rocket power.

Life was consistently enlivened by many small traditional celebrations or customs and buildings and streets were hung with displays of gaily coloured and intricate paper decorations to brighten the days. We always knew when a Chinese wedding took place, as cavalcades of cars, each decorated with large red paper hearts would drive through the streets of the town blasting their horns, escorting the bride and groom on the first journey of their married life.

Thaipusam Festival
Silver chariot bearing Lord Subramaniam to Hindu Temple

Thaipusam Festival
Bullocks pulling the chariot

Man with Kavahdi of spears

Kavahdi man taking a rest

Hindu woman with pierced cheeks Thaipusam Festival 1957

Chingay Festival Flags

Chingay procession decorated trishas. Penang 1957

Lion dance. Chingay procession. Penang 1957

Train bringing Father Christmas to RAF Butterworth 1956

Father Christmas arrives and is greeted by the station master (Harry).
RAF Butterworth 1956

Engine driver Jim Smith and station master Harry Page. RAF Butterworth 1956

Penang water festival. Spectators ashore. June 1956

Water festival 1956. Dragon Boat Race

Water festival. Pillow fight 1956

Chingay balancing act, Penang

CHAPTER NINE
Wildlife

The Natural wildlife in Malaya was all around us in abundance. Nice and nasty! Among the nice things were the great variety of birds and butterflies. Birds generally did not possess the lovely songs of those we hear in Britain, but I remember with pleasure the burbling call of the Bulbuls outside my bedroom window each morning. The black and yellow plumage of the Golden Oriole, the black zig-zag pattern on the wings of Fairy Blue Birds and the soaring flight of the Fish Eagles above the bright blue water are all pictures I bring to mind.

Large butterflies of many colours floated and flitted among the trees and undergrowth during the day and at night equally large moths took their place.

One evening Harry and I were relaxing in our flat, the children asleep in their room. As usual our balcony sliding doors were wide open to obtain maximum air and we were both engrossed in reading, when from the corner of my eye, I noticed a fluttering movement. At first I thought it to be a bird or a bat, but when it became entangled in the lampshade I saw it was a huge Atlas Moth. It had a wingspan of about eight inches across and was coloured of the most beautiful shades of red, russet, orange and brown. We watched and admired it for a few minutes before taking pity on its plight and turning off our light, allowing it to disentangle itself from the lampshade. This it did and we watched it float off towards the attraction of the street lamps opposite our home.

Among the nasties were the cockroaches, spiders, ants and snakes. The cockroaches were everywhere and it was necessary to turn out the cupboards and drawers frequently to dislodge them or they would eat their way through almost anything. They particularly liked certain shades of poster paint and children's paintings put on the wall one day would have holes eaten through them by next morning.. Spiders were my big horror. They were large hairy and jumped! Try to hit them and they would jump two feet away. Sometimes we watched a large cockroach and spider having a battle on the wall. Mostly the spider was the victor I think, but mostly I fled from the field of contest!

Ants were everywhere in sizes varying from the minute to two inches long. The larger ants were usually seen on the paths where the undergrowth flourished. I often saw a red ant and a black ant in single combat when I was on a walk out of town.

All homes had columns of ants trailing across the ceilings and down walls. There was no point in trying to eradicate the ants, as others would immediately take their place. They actually did a useful job in removing dead insects and other unwelcome remains and in so doing kept down the fly population by denying them opportunities for breeding.

Other useful little creatures in the home were the small gecko lizards that clung to the walls in strategic positions, often near a light, where they flicked up insects with their long sticky tongues. The bodies of these little lizards or 'chichak' were transparent and somewhat ghostly in appearance. Each chichak established its own territory, attacking any other that unwittingly invaded it. They usually led fairly peaceful and amiable lives except when they were stalked by our cat Ching. Ching waited for one to come within reach and then pounced, knocking the gecko to the floor. The gecko would then set its defence mechanism into action and usually escaped, leaving its discarded tail wriggling in the cat's paws while the gecko rapidly scaled the wall to a safer height.

A story that caused amusement among the 'old hands' of the expatriate population, was of a young wife newly arrived in Singapore who suddenly let out a scream for help, yelling that there was a wild animal in her room. Such a thing was possible and people went running to help. They found the husband with a roll of newspaper in hand dashing madly over beds and chairs, hitting out at an inoffensive little gecko that scampered quickly over walls and ceiling in an effort to evade him. Explanations were made and fears calmed, leaving the couple a little shamefaced, but with a story to laugh over later.

The Malay people, we were told, will not live in a house unless there are chichaks in it.

There are 129 different kinds of snakes in Malaysia. At least 20 varieties are poisonous. Luckily we saw very few of them. Mostly they try to avoid contact with humans, sliding away when they feel people approaching and all you see is a movement in the grass. Cobras do occasionally turn up in someone's bathroom or on a garden path and will attack. We knew one young lad who saved a neighbour's child from a cobra bite. The toddler was playing in the garden when it disturbed a cobra. The cobra instead of retreating raised its hood to strike. The fifteen-year-old boy grabbed a carving knife and sliced off the snake's head before it had time to strike the child. We heard tales of King Cobras chasing men on bicycles, but how much was fact and how much fiction, I do not know.

I do remember one occasion in our group of flats that caused a stir. A snake was found in a crate of beer delivered to one of the flats. The amah was putting a bottle in the cupboard when the snake moved. The amah screamed and fled, Mem who was ironing in the kitchen, jumped over the balcony, luckily on the ground floor, putting as much distance between her and the snake as possible. Somebody fetched the Kabun (gardener) who searched and found the snake and killed it to the accompanying squeals of the amahs. The snake was about three feet long and black in colour. When I looked it up in my book I discovered it to be a Common Malayan Racer snake. Non-poisonous! Another friend discovered a green snake behind his wardrobe and disposed of it out of his window. That turned out to be a tree snake also non-poisonous.

Most people killed first and asked questions afterwards, as some snakes were highly dangerous. The most lethal of all were the sea snakes for which there was no antidote. We knew someone who was bitten whilst playing ball with a group of friends in shallow water. He died within four hours. We never went swimming in the sea after this incident, but we heard of several other deaths from sea snake bites. Strangely enough, the local fishermen did not seem to be affected, although they often had a snake among their catch when they brought up their nets. They simply picked up these long, flat tailed, grey green creatures and threw them back into the sea.

While staying at Maxwells Hill rest house near Taiping we watched a young man catch a snake with the aid of a long, flexible bamboo pole. He was careful to keep his distance from the snake and so did we. So I never discovered what sort of snake it was.

Like all other creatures snakes have their uses helping to keep the rat population under control. The largest of all snakes in Malaya are the Pythons, as thick as a man's leg and up to fifteen feet or more long, they are beautifully patterned and non-poisonous. Occasionally one roamed through the RAF camp at Butterworth and a few pet dogs disappeared, as the pythons diet was not confined to rats. Pythons in search of a meal were even known to tackle a goat in the villages.

In RAF Butterworth in 1956 was a young National Serviceman who had been a keeper at London Zoo. He obtained permission to keep his own small private zoo on the camp. His main interest was in snakes and his collection provided a useful study centre. Jennifer and Virginia showed great interest and were allowed to hold some of the harmless varieties, finding instead of the slimy feel they were expecting, the skins of the snakes actually felt quite silky and pleasant.

Snake Charmers set up their acts with their baskets of coiled snakes wherever they found a suitable audience. One arrived on Christmas morning in the compound of our flats and proceeded to entertain the children with two hooded cobras, from which I suspect the fangs had been removed. Other Charmers used other snakes, such as large black and yellow-banded Mangrove Snakes. Should a householder be troubled by snakes in his garden, the snake charmer would come to cast his spell and entice them out by playing his music on a gourd like serunei instrument. He would then capture the snake and cut out its fangs before imprisoning it in his basket.

Snakes of various kinds could also be seen in the Snake Temple in Penang, lying about the building in a state of torpor, probably induced by the overpowering smell of burning incense. On the whole, more people died from falling coconuts than from snake bites.

On one extremely hot and humid week in March when the temperature was 95 degrees Fahrenheit, we rented a government bungalow on Penang Hill another 2,500 or more feet above sea level. The bungalow stood alone on the top of one small peak where sufficient ground had been levelled to provide it with a garden consisting of a lawn and flower borders. One end of the lawn came to an abrupt finish where cultivation ceased and natural vegetation took over on a slope that descended rapidly to a small roadway on a lower level some 50 feet or more down. When playing ball in the garden, care had to be taken if the ball was not to disappear down the hill in the dense undergrowth.

From this end of the lawn we had the most marvellous view. Dotted among the trees on the hillsides were the roofs of bungalows or houses of those lucky and wealthy enough to own homes in this cooler part of paradise. They could be reached only by the small cable railway, built in 1925, or a long laborious steep walk from the Moon Gate near Waterfall Gardens. For those on the hill these were the only means of connection with the noise, bustle and common necessity of work in the busy town below.

Here on the Hill all was peace and tranquillity, or so it seemed to us. It was not until the policeman called each evening to check that all was well that we realised we were still living in what the government termed a 'Black Area.' On the lower slopes we could see one or two Malay kampongs surrounded by clearer cultivated areas and further to our right the sheen of the reservoir that supplied the island's good clean water through its small but efficient pumping station.

Beyond all this and the intervening jungle lay Georgetown perched on the point of the island nearest to the mainland coast, its buildings standing white and stark against the dominant green of the vegetation on its land side and the brilliant blue of the water on its seaward side. In the straits between, ships waited at anchor to receive or discharge cargo and passengers, while others steamed on their way to ports further afield up and down the coast. The sound of the ship's sirens carried clearly to us, as we watched from the top of the hill. From our vantage point our eyes followed the ferry as it made its way across the channel to Prai on the mainland and looking into the greater distance we could see the misty high hill of Kedah Peak and the mountains that are the backbone to the coastal plain.

Standing in the cool clear air with only the sound of insects and birds around us and this wonderful panorama before us, was for me close to heaven. However even in such idyllic surroundings realism will intrude, and so it did that very first night.

After a pleasant meal provided by the resident Chinese cook and amah, a married couple who spoke little English, the children had been read their evening story, settled contentedly into their new bedroom and were soon asleep. Harry and I sat enjoying the cool evening and trying to identify the new sounds around us. There was always the familiar sound of the cicadas drumming out their insistent call and most evenings we heard the monotonous 'chook chook' call of the Night Jar bird, who repeated his single note again and again. I used to listen and count how many times it did this and found it could be as many as fourteen times before it took a rest.

Relaxed and cool we made our way to our room and prepared for bed. A slight noise caught my attention and I noticed a movement on the floor. Two bright eyes were watching me. It was a very large rat! I yelped with surprise. Harry decided he preferred not to share his bedroom with a rat and went in to attack. He tried to chase it out of the bungalow. The rat had other ideas and dived into the wardrobe. I shut the door on it. I reckoned that if we could not get it out, I wanted to know where it was. Also I was very tired and wanted to get to bed. We could tackle the rat in the morning.

Sleepily we climbed into our beds and turned out the light. That is when the cricket started chirping, and went on chirping very loudly! Meantime the rat had decided to try and gnaw its way out of the wardrobe. Between the gnawing of the rat and the continuous chirping of the cricket we found it almost impossible to sleep. We turned on the light. The cricket stopped chirping! We turned the light off. The cricket started chirping again. It seemed that the light was the signal. At least the light did not make a noise, so we decided to leave it on and dispense with the chirping, and hope the rat would give up on his gnawing! Eventually we were both so exhausted we fell asleep and were blissfully unaware for the rest of the night.

A lovely bright morning sun awoke us. Half asleep I made my way to the adjoining shower room and freshened up. As I came out Harry went in for his morning douche. Stark naked I reached into the wardrobe for clean clothes to find the rat only inches from my hand! I had completely forgotten it. I yelled and jumped back at least a yard. Harry came dashing out of the shower clad only in a towel. The rat sprang out of the wardrobe and ran under the bed. Grabbing a dressing gown, I yelled "Amah, Tekus, tekus" (rat,rat) Amah came running waving a broom, Jennifer and Virginia bounded in to see what all the noise was about, and there we all were, chasing one solitary rat all around the bedroom, the children jumping up and down on the beds with excitement, Harry desperately trying to preserve his decency with the towel and me watching where the rat ran and yelling directions to the amah who waved her broom at it valiantly. Eventually, the rat decided he had had enough of this game and fled into the shower room and out through the drainage pipe to the peace of the garden. I hurriedly stuffed the spiky lavatory brush into the drainage pipe to block any idea of a return visit. Calm was gradually restored.

At the end of the week we went to sign the visitors book and to our amusement found the rat to be a regular story, mentioned by most previous occupants. However we saw nothing of him for the remainder of our visit.

The best time to see the surrounding wild life was early in the morning. By simply sitting quietly in the garden or on the bungalow veranda, it was possible to see troops of monkeys bounding from one tree to another as they fed, or beautiful birds like the Fairy Bluebird, the blue of their plumage bright in the early morning light. The sight I found most exciting was watching the flying squirrels, much larger than I had expected, gliding from one tall tree to another, their limbs outstretched and the skin joining them acting as wings to their flight.

During the day it was cool enough to enjoy a walk and most of our days during this delightful week were spent exploring the paths on the hill. Many of these paths were lined with tall hedges of Bougainvillea, a mass of bloom in various tones of red and purple. Vast trees gave shade to other paths, and small bridges crossed chines in the hillside. Everywhere the vegetation was green and luxuriant. Plants grew so quickly that if not controlled and cut back regularly all paths would have soon disappeared.

On a spur of rock, high on the hill was a school. It provided, education and boarding for children of many of the European Planters and business men of Malaya, until children reached the age when it was necessary to send them home to Europe for further education. Isolated from life in the town, hemmed in by jungle on one side and surrounded by steep rocky hillsides on the other three, I wondered how the staff and children managed to keep themselves fully occupied.

The days passed all too quickly for us. The time came to say goodbye to cook and amah and return to work. Jennifer and Virginia looked forward to the ride down the hill in the cable railway. Monkeys crossed the tracks in front of the slow moving car, not hurrying on their way but often pausing to pick up some interesting morsel beside the cable. There were several stops at small hillside stations, but not many passengers as the two compartments together probably accommodated no more than twenty people. Apart from our own family there were only three other passengers at this time.

Halfway down the hill on a double stretch of track, we passed the other cars going up, all travelling at a very leisurely pace. The views decreased in distance and the heat increased in humidity until we were back once more at the base station, our short holiday over.

Penang Hill cable railway

Snake Charmers

and snakes at The Lone Pine Hotel, Penang

Georgetown from Penang Hill

Waterfall Botanical Gardens, Penang

Feeding the monkeys, Botanical Gardens, Penang

The greedy monkey, Botanical Gardens

CHAPTER TEN

Meetings with other creatures.

Lizards of many kinds abounded in Malaya, varying in size from the huge iguanas up to six feet from nose to tail tip, to the tiny chichaks on our walls.

One of the large iguanas crossed the road in front of our car, causing Harry to brake suddenly when we were driving some friends around the island one day. It was easy enough to imagine the dragons of medieval stories when looking at this monster. Long, squat and evil looking it moved surprisingly quickly across the road and into the bushes before we had a chance to get out of the car.

When Harry tried to start the car again the engine did not respond. There appeared to be a blockage in the petrol feed. It took about half an hour before it coughed back into life and we were able to set off once more. We managed about another fifteen miles before the engine died on us again. Our concern grew when this time we could get no response at all. Here we were, stuck far out in the middle of rural Penang in the middle afternoon, miles from any form of help and most unlikely to meet any other travellers. What was worse was that our friends were on route from Singapore to England and their ship was leaving Penang that evening.

Tinkering with the engine brought forth no results except to get the men covered in grease. Luckily the car had stopped on a downward slope at the top of the last hill leading to the flat coastal area. It was a road full of fairly sharp bends and a steep descent of 2,000 or more feet. We felt there was no alternative but to coast downhill as carefully as possible and trust that luck was on our side.

Back in the car, Harry released the brake and we started moving down the slope. It was an eerie sensation to be moving down this mountain road without the sound or vibration of the engine, rather like freewheeling on a bicycle. By keeping a hold on the brake and taking the bends with extra care, Harry brought us safely down to the last turn where the road ran down through a Malay kampong to the non-precipitant roads of the inner coastal plain. As he negotiated the bend he turned on the ignition. Much to everyone's great relief the engine roared into life and we completed the journey returning our friends to their ship all in good time.

Tree Lizards were frequently seen at close quarters, too close for a friend of mine. Wearing a dress with a wide necked cowl type of collar, she was walking through a coconut plantation one day when she felt something drop down the back of her dress inside the collar. Somewhat apprehensive, but disinclined to strip then and there, she hurriedly made her way to her rooms. On taking off her dress she discovered the cause of her anxiety. It was a large green tree lizard that had surprisingly lost its grip and found a soft landing place in the folds of my friend's dress. Considering that my friend had no knowledge of what nasties she might be harbouring, I think she showed great coolness and presence of mind in acting as she did.

One day I noticed our cat had caught something in the garden and went to look. It was a flying lizard with bright red spots dotting the green membrane of skin between its legs. This skin was supported by extended rib bones hinged to the backbone. Zenna was very concerned when I tried to pick it up, saying "Poison Mem" but I could find no evidence of it being poisonous when I consulted my book. It was about eight inches long.

Other animals could also give unexpected and alarming surprises. Harry was teaching in his school one day when an elephant thrust its head through the open window! Harry was involved in some work at the time. It was not until the restlessness of the children alerted him that something unusual was happening, that he looked up and saw the huge head and waving trunk filling the window frame. The elephant was not aggressive, just very curious. It had broken away from a team of working elephants passing down the road and wandered into the school grounds. Its loss was soon discovered and its Mahout returned to claim it and lead it away.

In another heart stopping incident, a family travelling by car to Kuala Lumpur had a close up view of a tiger that used the roof of their car as a jumping board to bound from one high bank to another! Tigers did occasionally turn man-eater and we sometimes saw in our newspapers that one had carried off a rubber tapper who had been working on trees on an estate.

Gibbons were popular pets with some people; they certainly seemed very affectionate animals and with their long arms clung to the necks and shoulders of their owners. The Orang Utang, whose name means 'Man of the Jungle' in Malay, is indigenous to Malaya. I was never lucky enough to see one in its wild state, but only in the zoo of the Sultan of Jahore. Its large mournful eyes and languid movement as it reached for the banana we offered gave a doleful appearance.

Minor Birds we saw everywhere. They were cheeky enough to take the food from your plate should you choose to eat outside. Although we never found one who would talk to us, like parrots, they could mimic sounds.

Small animals could cause strange happenings. One morning children were assembled for the morning hymn, the teacher at the piano awaiting the signal to play, when all at once the keys of the piano started to go up and down on their own volition. Prayers and hymns were suspended while the cause was investigated. When the back was taken off the piano, a small mouse was discovered running up and down the hammers of the keys. With mouse removed, assembly continued, almost as usual!

When the wet season arrived, a huge puddle formed just below our flat and here every evening as long as the puddle remained, toads and frogs gathered to do their courting. The various grunts, croaks and calls when put together sounded just like a creaking, rusty gate and with this sound we were serenaded every night until the rain clouds were blown away and the puddle dried up.

The Praying Mantis were intriguing if ungainly insects. They measured about three inches long in size and were green in colour. Their stiff careful movements and patient statuesque, absolutely still pose whilst awaiting the unwary fly gave plenty of opportunities for study. When in Ceylon, (now Sri Lanka) on night watch, one had often stationed itself on my desk close to the light where it obtained a regular feast from the attracted insects. The females have some very nasty habits; one of them is eating the male Praying Mantis after they have mated.

Brightly coloured; tiny fish inhabited the long open water filled ditches that lined some of the roads. The children had fun in netting some of them for an aquarium we made in a large glass carboy. The beaches provided pieces of coral and attractive shells, that when well washed in fresh water were placed in the bottom of the carboy and to these plants, also found in the ditches were added. The aquarium turned out to be an interesting and absorbing hobby. The whole family enjoyed learning to identify the different fish and watching their behaviour. Later we were able to add one or two more spectacular breeds to our collection such as the beautiful and brightly coloured male Siamese Fighting Fish with its flowing fins and tail. This did not come from the ditches, but was bought from one of the Chinese shops in town.

As in all areas where the British settled, Penang had its Botanical Garden. Known as Waterfall Gardens, it was an attractive Park at the foot of high hills below a waterfall from where the garden had its name. Bisected by a small stream it was carved from the surrounding jungle. The jungle was the home of many monkeys and other wild creatures. The monkeys became very bold soon realising that where there were people there would also be food. Groups of them sat on low branches of trees, the braver members of the troops venturing on to the open grass areas and up to the holidaymakers having their picnic.

To feed the monkeys, people brought bags of nuts and bunches of the small golden bananas. It was an activity enjoyed by our girls. On one occasion Virginia was offering some young animals nuts, feeding them one nut at a time. They were rather timid and hesitated before taking courage to come close enough to grab the nut. They then retreated to a safe distance to eat. This was all going along very nicely, keeping both the monkeys and Virginia fully occupied, but it was obviously not to the satisfaction of one large old monkey, who, scattering the young animals stalked straight up to Virginia, ignored the proffered singe nut, grabbed the bag from her left hand and proceeded to squat down and eat the lot. Leaving Virginia startled and nonplussed. It would have been unwise to argue with him, as all these animals were completely wild and quite liable to attack at provocation. So we left him to enjoy his feast and went on our way.

In parts of Malaya, mostly on the East Coast states such as Kelantan, monkeys were trained to work by some Malays. The monkey, or Berok as it was called, was trained to climb a coconut palm and select ripe nuts that it would remove and throw down to its owner. The Berok was attached to a long lead to prevent its escape should it take a fancy to independence.

When there were people around in the Gardens, most of the other wildlife very sensibly remained in the jungle and was not seen, but there was no doubt that it was about. Parties of hunters were sometimes given permission to shoot wild boar in the Botanical gardens when they became too destructive. Three wild boars were shot here in 1956.

True to British Tradition, the gardens possessed an attractive bandstand, and it was here people gathered to enjoy a relaxed hour or two, listening to selections of music by the bands of one of the regiments serving in Malaya at the time. The residential Malayan Police and the Federation regiment bands also took their turn along with the municipal band in entertaining the population in the cooler hours of the late afternoon.

CHAPTER ELEVEN
Journeys by Car to Alor Star and Singapore

Alor Star was a name that conjured up for me a romantic vision of the Orient. I knew nothing about it, except as a name seen on a map. According to this map it was only sixty miles or so to the north of us, on the mainland not far from the Thailand border and in the State of Kedah. Now that we had our own transport we could explore and I suggested to the family that it would make a good day out to go there.

Joined by our friend Bob (headmaster of the Army School in Penang), we set off early one morning to take the ferry to the mainland and head north. With only one slight setback when the engine gave a little trouble, but was fixed by Harry without too much loss of time, we drove on a straight road past padi fields and rubber plantations to Sungei Patani and enjoyed a refreshment break at the Rest House. Government Rest Houses were situated in most of the towns along the routes in Malaya and were a great boon to travellers. The caretakers of these useful establishments were always most helpful and able to produce refreshments at any time of day. Most Rest Houses were built in the old colonial style with cool lofty rooms and plenty of space. Accommodation was provided and bedrooms were usually large, provided with chairs and tables and own bathroom or shower and toilet. All rooms had ceiling fans.

A canal ran alongside the road on the last twenty miles to Alor Star part of the irrigation network that caused Kedah to be known as the rice bowl of Malaya. Apart from a few bullock carts and occasional car the road was free of traffic.

I am not quite sure what my imagination had led me to expect, but Alor Star, capital of the State of Kedah, turned out to be a quiet, well-spaced town with some very large public buildings and a beautiful Mosque. An impressive gateway stood at the entrance to the Sultan's Palace that was surrounded by a high wall. The population here was predominantly Malay and the atmosphere quiet and rural. Another and very large Rest House provided an excellent lunch and further energy to enjoy a leisurely wander around the area. Jennifer had ample opportunity to use her newly acquired camera, before we made our return journey to Penang arriving home about 7pm as darkness fell.

This short trip encouraged us to make further journeys, and in the following long holidays we took the girls on an extended trip to Singapore. The journey to Singapore from Penang as the crow flies is about five hundred miles, but we were in no hurry and wished to see as much as possible of the country on the way. Using the Rest Houses for accommodation we planned our route and on August 13th 1956 left Penang for the mainland and the first fifty-eight miles of our journey to Taiping in the State of Perak. Taiping was a town that had a particular interest for me. When we had told my parents that we intended to work in Malaya, my father had searched out an old photograph among the family snapshots. It showed an uncle of his among a group of Malay men. The photograph was taken at the beginning of the 20th century in the town of Taiping, where this uncle, another roving relative, was something to do with organising the registry office there. Uncle had long since departed this world, but never the less had left behind him an intangible feeling of some connection for me.

Although on a branch of the main north-south route, Taiping, was not a large or busy market town and we had explored it on a previous journey. This time our aim was to spend two nights in the refreshingly cooler atmosphere of Maxwells Hill 3,600 ft. above sea level. To do this we garaged our car with the Taiping Rest House and took the two-dollar trip in the Land Rover transport required to negotiate the twists and turns of the steep, narrow road up.

The Rest House on the top of the hill was spacious cool and comfortable. The views were tremendous extending over dark green jungle covered hills to the cultivated plain or glinting water of the sea dotted with misty islands. When the sun set at close of day, by sitting on the veranda we could enjoy a kaleidoscope of colour, followed by a soft black night sky in which the brilliant stars outshone the twinkling lights of the town far below.

In the delightful freshness of this higher altitude we took advantage of some walks in the vicinity of the Rest House where we saw many butterflies of different colours, one particularly large one that we at first mistook for a bird as it flitted among the lush undergrowth. It was here where we saw a Chinese boy catch a small brown snake and carry it up the hill curled around the end of the boy's bamboo pole.

Two nights here restored our energy and emboldened us to travel on to the next stop on our itinerary, the quiet port of Lumut, still in Perak. To do this we had to pass Trong and deviate from the main highway on to a branch road at Bruas that ran through the flat area of the Dindings. The section of the road from Trong to Bruas was a series of continual s-bends winding in and out of rubber plantations. In contrast, the road through the Dindings was long straight and lonely. We saw only two or three other cars on the whole of this stretch of our journey passing through Ayer Tawar.

Lumut was a quiet backwater on the flat coastal plain with few buildings and seemingly even fewer people. We walked along its narrow beach looking for shells and giving the girls an opportunity of freedom from the confinement of the car.

From Lumut we had intended to visit Pankor Island where in World War II members of Task Force 136 were landed by submarine in order to infiltrate behind Japanese Lines and collect information and encourage harassment by guerilla fighting. Spencer Churchill writes of their activities in his book 'The Jungle is Neutral'. The island is also known as the site where a Peace Treaty, was signed by the Governor Sir Andrew Clark with the Sultan of Perak in 1874. A photograph of the Governor and his staff hung on the wall in the Rest House at Lamut.

Apart from its historical associations, Pankor Island was and probably still is, very beautiful. Unfortunately we did not manage to get there due to a rainstorm in which we took a wrong road and a second storm which caused a traffic hold up. These incidents caused us to be too late to get a launch out to the island and back before dark.

A scene that had intrigued us on our journey occurred after the rainstorm. Some of the roads were lined with small canals and in these we noticed a number of men and boys fishing , using large square nets suspended from long bamboo poles. I would have been interested to know what they hoped to catch, but as we were already late there was no time to stop and enquire

So far apart from the storms, the journey had been easy. The few main roads Malaya possessed were well maintained and had rubberised McAdam surfaces that made travelling relatively smooth. There were the occasional hold ups when we came to a check point barrier when all vehicles were obliged to stop and be searched by soldiers or police. This was to prevent people carrying any food or weapons that might get into the hands of the terrorists. Since the policy of 'New Towns' or 'New Villages' had been introduced the Communist Terrorists (CTs) had found it harder to obtain supplies. Before the 'New Town' policy, apart from the Malay people, who usually lived in Kampongs that were fairly compact and easier to guard, other people lived spread in sparsely populated areas over the countryside with no protection and were easy prey for the CTs in their demands for food and supplies. By gathering these people together and enclosing them in 'New Villages' protected by high wire fences and armed guards, the authorities made life much more difficult for the terrorists. Although free to come and go during the day, at night the gates would be shut and the inhabitants enclosed behind the wire, hopefully secure against attack.

After one night in Lumut Rest House, we set off once more to make our way south. To rejoin the main highway it was necessary to retrace our route as far as Bruas and turn eastward over the large metal bridge spanning the Perak river, on the Batu Gajah, a Malay name meaning Elephant Rock. Apart from a cinema with walls painted bright blue and covered with lurid posters there was little to take our interest here, but the Rest House was pleasant and their coffee good. The road now became hilly and winding. Bordered in many places by thick jungle we were relieved to know that the country between here and Kuala Lumpur was considered a 'White Area' and therefore unlikely to be subject to terrorist ambush.

In sections where the jungle had been cleared, rubber trees had been planted in neat rows following the contour of the land. Occasionally there were clearer patches where old trees had been cut down and replaced with new saplings. Rubber trees when tapped for latex normally lasted fourteen years. The Tappers visiting each tree twice a day. First early in the morning when a V shaped cut was made on the trunk and a small bowl shaped cup positioned at the point of the V and then again some hours later to collect the latex that had accumulated in the cup.

Stopping only at Tapah for lunch, or 'tiffin' as it was called, that

Harry noted as 'very poor', we drove on through the large tin mining area of Rawang where the soil had been washed into murky lakes in which the dredgers were at work.

On the northern outskirts of Kuala Lumpur we passed through Templer Park named after Lady Temple, wife of the former High Commissioner of the Federation Sir Gerald Templer. Here the natural vegetation closes in on the road and gradients combined with bends required concentration on the drivers part. About fifteen miles outside Kuala Lumpur are the Batu Caves, strange towers of limestone rock that stand out like sentinels from the surrounding countryside. More solid than their accompanying hills that time has eroded; these outcrops of limestone have been left as land marks at random intervals along the way from Kuala Lumpur to Ipoh. Many of the caves that they contain have been adapted as shrines and pilgrims go to pay respect to their various gods.

The 207 miles from Lumut to Kuala Lumpur went well. Our only moment of unease was when we had to stop for petrol at the village of Trolak in the middle of a 'Black Area'. The village was surrounded by barbed wire and when we asked for petrol we had the feeling that we were definitely unwelcome. There were no smiles or conversation, but rather hostile stares. One became used to being stared at in the Far East, but here we started to get that creepy feeling down the spine and were glad to pay the bill and move on as quickly as possible.

Eventually we reached Kuala Lumpur, a thriving city with much traffic and a complicated one way system in which we promptly got lost. Having got ourselves stuck in the wrong lane of traffic we had to find our way back to starting point by continually turning right. Our arrival at the rest house was experienced with triumph and much relief and for the next two days we left the car and took to 'shanksese's pony' and the occasional trisha for negotiating the streets of Kuala Lumpur.

Facing the main Padang in Kuala Lumpur were and possibly still are, the elaborate and attractive buildings of the administration and a little further down the road, the magnificent railway station, built like a palace and all for two trains a day. Kuala Lumpur being the Capital City of Malaya had many fine buildings, one of the most beautiful being the main mosque with its delicate domed roof and minarets. Looking as though it had come straight from the stories of the Arabian Nights on a magic carpet and placed on the apex of land where the rivers Klang and Gombak meet, so that it was surrounded by water on two of the three sides of the triangle.

The shopping centre was bigger than that of Penang, with more large European stores displaying reasonably up to date fashions and goods. Robinsons Store contained a most attractive air- conditioned café where we enjoyed delicious iced coffees while cooling off.

One of the drawbacks of travelling on the mainland was the mosquito that attacked us at night. On Penang Island we had very few problems with these annoying insects and never needed to use a mosquito net. My first night at Kuala Lumpur was a misery. I awoke about 3am realising I had been badly bitten by these little pests and found some of them sharing my net tent. As it was impossible to sleep through their high- pitched whine dive bombing attacks; I turned on the light and spent the next hour or two trying to catch the horrors. Anyone who has suffered a similar fate will know how infuriating that can be! With no solid walls to squash them against, confined within an entangling net with many folds in which they can hide and endeavouring not to loosen the net in case further reinforcements of these little sharp nosed horrors slipped in, is not an easy task. My enemies finally eliminated, I settled down to snatch what chance of sleep was left to me, willing myself not to scratch the wounds of my battle.

On our second day in Kuala Lumpur I wrote to my parents of our journey so far and noted "There is a terrific storm on at the moment, bags of lightening and thunder which shakes the table on which I write". Luckily, tropical storms such as this were usually short lived and the sun soon returned to dry out the streets once more.

Some friends I had made on board the ship out arrived at the rest house to invite us out to dinner on the second evening of our stay. Having arranged for an amah to stay with the children, Harry and I went with Joyce and her husband, an engineer in the tin mining industry. They took us to the 'Griffin' a most attractive restaurant in Kuala Lumpur the food was as delicious as the building was attractive with many varieties of both Eastern and Western dishes from which to choose. To add to this a small orchestra played music for dancing, while a cool night breeze gently blew through the open sides of the building. A most pleasant way to spend a few relaxing hours.

Like myself Joyce was adapting to life as a wife and mother in tropical conditions. Her young son attended a British Army School with five other young children of European civilian workers from the same area that all travelled the 20 miles into school each day. She was expecting a second child and found the heat somewhat trying but appreciated the fact that we had amahs and cooks to remove the burden of housework and cooking over a hot stove. This freedom gave much more time for socialising. Many women were happy to take advantage of this while they could and became involved in Bridge Parties, coffee mornings and entertaining guests or being guests at dinner parties and other functions. Some, and I was one, found the social round too demanding and opted out to a certain degree by taking a job. If paid jobs were hard to come by, there were always some voluntary jobs to do, such as I had found with the Red Cross. One or two women managed to find work with the radio station; another ran the AA Malaya motoring organisation in Penang in conjunction with her Chinese husband. Others, like myself were teaching or nursing. It was not necessary to be idle unless you wished to be so.

Those interested in the craft of needlework had a galaxy of wonderful fabrics from which to choose, all easily available in their local stores. Beautiful silks and brocades from China and Thailand, batiks from Indonesia and Malaya, cool cottons from Egypt and India, chiffons, satins, raw silk, linen, just about every type of material that had ever been woven were to be had for the asking. Also on sale was the new man made fabric, nylon. It was light and alluring in many different shades, but we soon discovered that its diaphanous folds were unsuitable for tropical climates as its close weave was stifling to the body and did not allow the skin to breathe. There was plenty of choice in the lovely natural fabrics to keep us busy for years. Most of my own dresses were made by local seamstresses who required no pattern, but simply a picture as a guide and from this produced a model dress. However I made all the children's dresses. These were simple cotton affairs mostly as with the unvaryingly hot climate nothing warmer was required. Due to the heat and continual washing and changing, quite a large number of dresses were needed for they were soon worn out.

Before leaving Kuala Lumpur we bought some pillows for the children to use in the car. They had found the last part of our trip of over 200 miles rather tiring for them and consequently wearing for us, as they became more irritable. The pillows helped to solve the problem as when tiredness or boredom set in they simply went to sleep.

As it happened the next stage of our journey was a short one, only 43 miles to Seremban where we planned to stop for lunch, but the way was through a notoriously bad 'Black Area'. The jungle enclosed the road for some way beginning only 15 miles south of Kuala Lumpur. Being a very winding road also, it made an ideal area for an ambush. Between Semenyih and Seremban were numerous checkpoints manned by troops and police. We were pleased to arrive in Seramban safely and relax in the attractive Rest House for a welcome lunch.

From Seramban it was another short trip of only 21 miles to the coast and Port Dickson. As the Rest House was already full, we booked into the Si-Rasa Inn, a Chinese Hotel. Our room contained one huge bed under a vast mosquito net. It seemed that there were no other beds or rooms available, so we ended up all four of us in a row under this great muslin drapery reminding one of the Great Bed of Ware, in days of yore. At least we had the advantage of knowing our fellow travellers.

Our rest was not greatly helped by the activities of an Asian Youth Camp situated just outside our bedroom window. The most popular amusement appeared to be talent contests with the aid of a loudspeaker system and this they maintained until the late hours of the night. Harry was uncharitable enough to wish it would pour with rain and drown their efforts!

The hotel also boasted a juke- box in the garden, again a popular past- time with the young. Chinese pop music is no more melodic to European ears, than was the later 'Punk' music to the older generation. Between the Juke-box and the youth camp, sleep did not come easily to Harry and I, although the children were unaffected by the noise and were asleep almost immediately on getting into bed.

Our rising next morning was encouraged by the sound of a bugle, blown with great enthusiasm, if somewhat short of skill and we realised that next door to the youth camp and only a short distance further along the beach was a camp of Boy Scouts.

As it was then about 6am and further sleep was impossible, we donned our bathing costumes and went for an early morning swim. The beaches in Port Dickson were clean and the sea reasonably shallow and safe for children. Jennifer and Virginia could quite happily have spent all day there, but the thought of a second night in the hotel was too much for Harry and I. After breakfast we packed our bags and left on the next stage of our journey, I forgetfully leaving all our swimming costumes hanging on the line in the hotel's garden!

Apart from the good bathing facilities, the only other point to recommend our stay in Port Dickson, was the huge mound of Nasi Gorang we had for our evening meal. Cost being the equivalent of half a crown (2s 6d) in English money in those days or, 12,and a half p. on the decimal system. Nasi Gorang, literally translated is fried rice. It comes stuffed full of other tasty items such as prawns, egg and various pieces of meat and vegetables all combined together to make a filling and satisfying meal and was a great favourite with the family.

Having left Selangor, we had crossed the border about halfway between Kuala Lumpur and Seremban, we were now in the State of Negri Sembilam, heading towards Malacca and Malacca town, a distance of roughly 60 miles. I took over the driving to give Harry a rest and a chance to look at the scenery. The road was good in small patches, but very winding all the way. The first part of the road follows the coastline for a short distance before veering to take a loop inland and then returning to the coast.

We found the journey interesting as we passed through a number of neat Malay villages with beautifully carved and clean wooden attap houses, often with flowering shrubs and potted plants arranged outside or lining the path and steps to their door. A difference we noted to the Malay homes in Penang, were the attractive coloured tiles that formed the steps. It was an obvious influence of the early Portuguese occupation of Malacca. After these Malay houses, the shacks of the Chinese and Indian workers looked very shabby indeed.

In one of the kampongs or villages, we made a brief stop and asked permission of the schoolteacher to visit his school. He pleasantly agreed and invited us in. The building was similar in style to the attap houses, built on stilts to allow air to circulate underneath, but the single classroom had woven walls that reached only halfway towards the low overhanging eves of the thatched roof, the rest being open to the air. The class was a large one of nearly fifty pupils, all boys, and formally arranged in even rows behind individual desks. They were all attentive, polite and quiet in behaviour, at least while we were there. It would have been impossible for the schoolmaster to teach so many if they were not. There seemed to be little in equipment apart from the blackboard and easel and the books the children were using. As we did not wish to interrupt the lesson for too long, we gave our thanks and departed.

Our way now took us past many padi fields divided by small mud banks. In some of the fields water gleamed in the sun, in others the rice was pushing through its emerald green stems, standing straight and still in the humid air. In yet other sections, the farmer and his big grey and black water buffalo ploughed up the soil with a primitive single furrow wooden machine, the buffalo's strong shoulders, low slung head and wide horns straining to pull forward through the clinging mud, while behind, the farmer in his woven, wide brimmed protective hat guided his plough.

Rice growing in Malaya was done exclusively on the small holding system and produced about sixty per cent of the country's total needs. An average family could not tend more than seven acres with efficiency, but some holdings were very much smaller, often being less than one acre.

The rice takes from five to seven months to grow. Seed is planted and the seedlings transplanted after 30-40 days. This was done by the women. While the rice is growing the level of the water in the field is maintained to a depth of around eight inches. A few weeks before harvest the field is drained, allowing the crop to ripen. When ripe, the rice stalks were cut by hand and the seed beaten out and winnowed, again mostly by hand. Harvesting was a time when extra hands were needed and so was a communal activity when friends and neighbours gathered to help one another, much as they did in Europe before the invention of the combine harvester machine. This made an attractive and interesting scene for the idle watchers such as us, but hard, though sociable work for the harvesters.

Approaching the town of Malacca, the road followed the shore and provided a good place to stop and take a break from driving. The girls and I walked along the sandy shore looking for interesting shells and cooling our feet in the lapping water while Harry settled himself on the bank and chatted to a Malay man who was also resting there.

This man wore a white cap that denoted that he was a Haji and had been to Mecca on pilgrimage. To go to Mecca was the ambition of every Muslim man, but as the cost was in the region of $2000 Malayan dollars, it often involved saving up for many years to afford the fare. There were about two ships a year that sailed from Singapore and Penang, taking hundreds of pilgrims from Malaya to Mecca. The quayside became a thronged mass of pilgrims and their families, come to see their men off on the greatest and most important journey of their lives. For this momentous occasion the women wore their finery and filled the watersides with splashes of bright colour.

In the shallows of this sandy Malacca shore the girls and I watched men wading pushing something before them under the water. At intervals they stopped and from beneath the calm sea a huge triangular net attached to a bamboo frame, at least twice as large as the man, slowly appeared. This they inspected closely before lowering it once more and resuming their wading. We assumed they were doing the equivalent of shrimping.

Malacca was the most interesting of all the towns visited on our journey. It was of course the most historical, some of its buildings dating from the occupation of the Portuguese who built a settlement here in 1490. On the hill are the remains of the fort built by Don Alfonso d'Albuqureque to guard the settlement and in the gardens on the sea front on land reclaimed from the sea is a rock on which stands a cross, symbolic of the one planted by his men.

Descendants of the early Portuguese who intermarried with Malays and Chinese, still spoke a patois called "Lingua de Christao" and celebrated the Feast of St. Peter in their settlement at Ujong Pasir with folk songs, dances and music of old Portugal.

On the South West Coast on the mouth of a river, Malacca was an ideal position for a trading port. Its advantages were noticed by the Dutch who in the 17th century overthrew the Portuguese and established their own trading port here. Much of the old town dates from this time and styles of buildings are reminiscent of those seen in the Netherlands, such as the Stadthuis, and Christchurch, built in the 18th century and the houses backing on to the wharves where the merchant ships were loaded with the spices and silks of the Far East. The old and narrow streets provided further reminders in the names. Jonkheer Street and Heeren Street. On the hill stood the ruin of the church of St. Paul, built in 1520 whose remaining walls were lined with gravestones of long-dead sea captains and merchants. Christian pilgrims still climbed the many steep and narrow steps to visit these ruins, for it was here in St. Paul's Church that St. Francis Xavier, Apostle to the Indies was buried before the site of the high alter. Later his remains were exhumed and reburied in Goa, a country far from Malaya. A statue of St.Francis stood on the hill overlooking old Malacca.

As we drove over the bridge into the centre of the old town we seemed to be surrounded in a rosy glow, quite unconnected with any form of alcohol. The glow arose from the buildings around us. Built in a red laterite clay that appears to harden with the passing years, they were painted in a rich terracotta colour on which the sun poured its rays to produce this pinkie haze.

Some of these sturdy buildings have walls six feet thick and must have provided a welcome defence in troubled times as well as excellent insulation against the heat of the tropical sun. Although the ancient walls of the old town no longer stood to enclose the settlement area, one gateway remained. Its carved stone symbols and coat of arms reminding one of past splendours

After the Dutch came the British who acquired Malacca during the aftermath of the Napolionic wars of the early 19th century. The British continued to use Malacca as a trading port, but in the 1950's its future as such did not look too bright as the slow flowing river was gradually causing the silting up of the port.

Our room at the Rest House was very comfortable and very large accommodating the four of us easily. We also had our own bathroom and toilet and a balcony veranda where we could sit in the evenings and enjoy the cool sea breezes.

One of the old Dutch houses had been turned into a local museum and proved most interesting. The house stood in Fort Terrace. It had the reputation of being haunted. Many eerie tales were connected with it, but we noticed no ghostly happenings when we explored its dark and cool interior. Apart from its antique Dutch furniture the house held remnants of the history of Malacca, the gong that summoned the Malay soldiers to battle, blowpipes and bark canoe of the Sakai or aboriginal peoples of Malaya, weapons, children's carriages and musical boxes. One section of the Museum was devoted to objects used in the celebration of a Chinese wedding of a hundred or so years before. The wedding costumes of the bride, groom, and young attendant were all covered in the most exquisite embroidery in brilliant colours that still retained their lustre in spite of the passing years. The Bridal bed, painted bright red, a colour denoting good luck and happiness was inlaid with hundreds of pieces of mother of pearl shell in elaborate designs as was the furniture in the room. Ornaments and jewellery, ornate and colourful also had their place.

Jennifer was intrigued with all the exhibits, but Virginia failed to be impressed until we reached the section housing the stuffed animals, butterflies and snakes, then at last her attention was captured.

Outside the museum were a number of short posts. On these posts rested some wooden saucer shaped discs containing a coil of thick rope. These were 'Main Gasing' or Spinning tops. Top spinning was a traditional sport of Malay men in kampongs in much of Malaya and the skills of those who showed the greatest expertise were greatly admired. The hardwood disc is about the size of a dinner plate, it is highly polished and sometimes rimmed with steel. The spindles are frequently surrounded and decorated with Kelantan silver or even gold. One end of the rope is tied to a tree and the other end placed close on the spindle. The player then starts to wind the length of rope in tight, flat circles to the edge of the disc. After six turns the top is fully wound, the rope is released from the tree and tied around the player's wrist. He is then ready to throw.

A whiplike action with his arm and the top is sent spinning on the hard earth and will continue to spin for up to ten minutes. Those more skilled in the art are able to scoop up the top with a wooden bat and set it still spinning on a small post, or juggle it between two bats and even throw it from man to man while it continues to rotate at high speed.

Top spinning with British children appears to have gone out of fashion, but I can still remember the fun my friends and I had as children when the season for tops came around. In recent years I have seen the game still played by children in Spain, so it has not yet completely disappeared.

On our last evening in Malacca we took the girls to the Settlement Fair. Paying our entrance fee we walked among the crowds of a thousand people or more to explore its numerous attractions. Harry was magically drawn towards the section entirely devoted to food. The area was filled with a conglomeration of hawker's stalls from which aromas from delightfully appetising, to downright smelly issued forth. The food was cooked on the spot over little charcoal fires and was appreciated by a continual stream of customers.

It was possible to buy Satai, little cubes of meat on a long skewer dipped in a hot sauce and grilled over the charcoal fire. For each stick you were charged ten cents. The charcoal seemed to add extra flavour to the meat, making a tasty snack. Satai is a Malay speciality, but by moving to different stalls it was possible to try an assortment of foods from different cultures, Malay curries, the varied and delectable stir fry products of the Chinese wok cooking, or the hot spicy Indian dishes, all produced on portable charcoal stoves.

In a circle around the perimeter of the ground brightly lit by long neon tubular lighting were the stalls of various firms displaying their goods or advertising their services to the public view. The stalls I found most interesting were those in the centre circle of the fair demonstrating the arts and crafts of the people of Malaya. From coconut shell to Kalantan silver, the variety of goods was intriguing. Endless items were made from the plentiful coconut shells, bowls, spoons, back scratchers and other simple objects for everyday use: beautifully patterned woven mats were made from leaves and fibres; ornaments and handles made from polished black buffalo horn. Delicate silver work and jewellery worked by silversmiths into many designs and beautiful objects. Embroidery and paintings added colour and further interest. Models of fish traps, houses and ships neatly and painstakingly carved and put together in fascinating detail.

There were of course entertainments and demonstrations for the crowds and we stayed to see a puppet show before taking the children back to the Rest House and bed. On asking the girls if they had enjoyed their day, the answer was "Oh yes, it was smashing and we were able to stay up late!"

Before leaving Malacca we had the car checked over at a local garage to make sure all was in good working order as the next part of our journey was to take us through a notorious Black Area not a healthy place to break down.

On the morning of the 18th August we started out, intending to reach Batu Pahat in the state of Johore in time for lunch. The drive as far as Muar, that we reached without incident was similar in aspect to that seen from Port Dickson to Malacca, very much Malay in character with traditional houses and distinctive bullock carts.

There was no bridge at Muar and in order to cross the river it was necessary to take a ferry.

The ferries consisted of flat- based barges that were pushed or towed across by a motor launch. The manoeuvring of an engineless barge loaded with lorries, cars and passengers against the river currents was a tricky business managed with skill by the vessel's pilot. The charges on the ticket for the ferry issued by Penambang Co. Muar make interesting reading to visitors from the west.

Lorry (empty) $2.50

Van with Lorry Frame (empty) $2.50

Lorry (empty) with Trailer (empty) $4.50

Motor Car $1.50

Van (small) $2,00

Motor Cycle $1.00

Bullock Cart $3.00

Bullock $1.00

6am to 6pm

On leaving the ferry we noticed that the car was not responding as well as it should do. We made our way to the Rest House and had coffee before going to find a garage. Having found a garage our next problem was to find someone who spoke English. This eventually achieved we discovered that the hand brake had slipped and the repair would take at least two hours. Leaving the car with the garage we returned to the Rest House to have lunch and wait. At about 2.30 the car was returned to us and we set off for Batu Pahat 33 miles further on. Just outside the town we passed a notice which proclaimed "You are now entering a Black Area. On no account stop for the next 80 miles."

We had travelled only about five of those miles when there was a sinking, lopsided feeling and then a series of bumps. We had a flat tyre! Despite the notice, there was nothing for it but to stop and change the wheel.

This was the first time either of us had ever changed a wheel and we did it in record quick time! Luckily no CTs appeared, nor did we see any other travellers so felt very much on our own, with the edges of the coconut plantations adjoining the road and only the coconuts for company. Having successfully completed the change we returned to Muar to get the puncture repaired. After a delay of about an hour we were ready to set off again and this time made our route through the coconut plantations without further trouble. The road was fairly straight most of the way and having negotiated one more ferry crossing we arrived safely in Batu Pahat. Apart from noticing that the town was quite a big one we had no time to see more. The journey had been hot and frustrating and we were keen to find the Rest House and a cool shower.

The Rest House turned out to be old and not too well kept, but as we only intended to spend one night there we did not let that bother us too much. Showered and refreshed, it did not take long for Jennifer and Virginia to find some Chinese children willing to join them in some skipping games. This kept them happily occupied until their evening meal and bed. As the girls were getting ready for bed, I noticed Jennifer looking very thoughtful. Suddenly she asked "Mummy are we very rich?" Surprised at such a question I said "Why do you ask?"

" The Chinese girl I was playing with said we were."

"Oh I see. I suppose compared to her life, the fact that we have a car and that you have nice clothes and toys would make you seem rich in her eyes."

Like many Chinese children this young girl of around Jennifer's age of eight years, was already taking a share of the family duties by being responsible for the care of several younger brothers and sisters while their parents were busy working. While she turned the skipping rope she carried a young baby of less than a year old straddled and held on her hip. To care for the younger siblings was an accepted way of life for elder children. I had noticed that quarrels or outbursts of temper among such groups were very rare. Any noisy disagreements and shows of ill temper heard were usually among the European children who were often spoiled not only by their parents but often by their amahs also.

Most European parents were able to afford to shower gifts upon their children, providing almost anything they asked for. In spite of this some children were dissatisfied and selfish in their behaviour and also extremely rude to their amahs and servants in general. More than once I had the urge to chastise a child for such discourteous behaviour.

Asian children apart from the more wealthy members of the community, appeared to have few manufactured toys but found their playthings in the simple and natural things around them or in discarded items such as old tins, and boxes. Nevertheless they appeared happy and if there were disagreements among them they were usually sorted amicably without the tears and rages displayed by many European children.

During the evening we chatted to an Eurasian couple who told us that the towns population was over 20,000. Muar was much smaller and although it had nicely laid out gardens along the river front and a few very attractive European houses, one police lieutenants wife I spoke to did not enjoy living there at all. Apparently it was very difficult to obtain European type food, especially bread that she could only get on two days a week. The rest of the time the family had to make do with the local bread that was very sweet, more like cake and generally not to European taste.

Even in Penang obtaining wheat flour could be a problem. It soon became infested with weevils that had to be sifted out before one could use it. Towards the end of our stay in Malaya, the firm of McDougalls began to export their flour in screw top plastic containers instead of paper sacks. This made a tremendous difference. We were then able to enjoy the benefit of wheat flour free of all these nasty little wriggling bodies. We could concentrate on keeping the ants out of the sugar instead!

We intended to make an early start next morning, but walked out to find yet another flat tyre. There must have been a slow puncture in the tyre we had changed. Harry decided to forgo his breakfast and concentrate on getting the car in order. Having changed the wheel and had the puncture repaired we finally moved off on the next stage of our journey about 10am.

From Ayer Hitam on, our route took us through designated Black Areas in which there were continual police checks at roadblocks. There were also large notices warning travellers not to stop on the road unless they had written permission from the District Officer. One stretch of this road about a mile long, consisted of very sharp, unrolled flints over which Harry drove with great caution fearful of yet another flat tyre.

Luck was with us and we made a safe arrival in the pleasant little town of Jahore Bahru. We drove along the wide road by the waterfront with its spacious green grass verges and shady trees to the most attractive new Rest House situated on a hill. From this charming position its guests obtained an excellent view of Singapore Island across the straits.

The Rest House was more expensive than the others we had been in, but was well worth it for the comfort it provided. Each double room cost $10 a night. We took two, one for the children and one for ourselves. Each room had twin beds with Dunlopillow mattresses, easy chairs and writing desks besides the normal bedroom furniture, there was also a telephone in every room. Each room also had its own bathroom tiled in blue and white with the latest type of shower and mixer taps. The children had the time of their life working all the knobs!

Such a description of the facilities of the rest house must sound quite mundane in present times of 2010, but in 1956 such luxury, even in hotels in Europe was comparatively rare. As we discovered on our return home to England when, journeying through Switzerland we stayed for several days at a hotel in Ascona and were charged extra for using the bath in the general bathroom for guests on that floor of the establishment.

To return to 1956 you will gather that we were most impressed by the standard of our accommodation. We also noted that the lounge and dining rooms were beautifully decorated, the Rest House gardens very attractive and the food was excellent. The only thing that spoilt this haven was a d…tom cat who sat outside our window and howled all night!

On the afternoon of our arrival in Jahore Bahru the clouds burst and the rain teemed down. To try and explore in such a downpour was out of the question, so we took the opportunity to rest. The following morning all was bright, clear and dry once more and ideal weather to visit the Istana Gardens Zoo owned by the Tenku, prince and eldest son of the then Sultan of Johore. The Tenku had gathered a collection of animals together in his grounds that he kindly opened to the public view.

The children enjoyed seeing real tigers, bears and many other animals and birds especially as we were able to feed some of them with small bananas and nuts. There were of course many tigers roaming in Malaya and stories of them featured frequently in the newspaper, but we had been fortunate enough not to have a close encounter with one up to now. Seeing them close at hand gave the children some understanding of how graceful as well as ferocious these majestic animals could be.

Having spent a relaxed hour or two in the Garden Zoo we returned to our car and drove the last few miles across the causeway onto Singapore Island, arriving at our friends home in Changi in time for lunch.

Changi was a name that had bad connotations and memories of the Japanese occupation for many people. Used as a prison camp it was the site of great hardships and regrettable atrocities. A neighbour of ours who had been nursing in Malaya when it was invaded had been imprisoned there, as also had a District Officer friend. The privations and difficulties were still too recent for the scars to have healed mentally if not physically and most people who had suffered in this way were still unwilling to talk about it.

In 1956 Changi was now a Royal Air Force base and a warm welcome awaited us from our weather friends Joan and Fred and their family. Our stay in Singapore was hectic but great fun. The contrast with the relaxed attitude to life that prevailed on Penang was stimulating but at the same time exhausting.

The city's six-lane traffic was horrendous and the drivers seemed completely mad. In spite of one way systems, traffic lights and ample space, in one evening in town we saw five accidents, mostly cars caught in monsoon drains after skidding or swerving and one nasty head on collision. The city being, even in 1956 a big commercial and trading centre was very prosperous. Its many large shops stocked with large selections of goods of the latest trends and designs. Beautiful clothes from the west, brocades, jade and jewellery from the east, wonderful carvings, camphor wood chests and so many other delights that had I an ever full purse I could easily have spent the whole four days in an ecstasy of shopping. As it was, the purse was a little low, particularly on our first two days there, as we had arrived too late to get to the bank before it closed for the weekend. We hoped that Fred would be able to see us through should we have any unexpected expense.

On the Saturday evening, having arranged for the Chinese amah to look after our girls, Fred and Joan took Harry and I to see some of Singapore's night spots. Our first call was at the Sea View Hotel a popular place for dinner and dancing on the sea front. The lounge and bar were all decorated with jungle motifs, the dividing screens and the furniture were of bamboo and all around the bar were faces carved from coconut shells. You could not get much more tropical! The theme for the restaurant deviated a little. Named Chicken Inn it was decorated with dozens of lanterns in the shape of chickens hanging from its ceiling. A dance band and singer provided music to enable patrons to sway or shuffle on the very small dance floor.

Perhaps the minute size of the dancing space encouraged the intimate, pleasant and happy relaxed atmosphere that prevailed here.

After a while our friends suggested we move on and pay a visit to the famous Raffles Hotel. In the car Harry broached the subject of our diminishing funds only to find that Fred was in a similar position until the banks reopened. It turned out that they had the equivalent of about 5 shillings each, 25p in present decimal currency. Having had a good laugh over the situation we elected to go to Raffles anyway, but Joan and I were restricted to one glass of orange juice each and our husbands to one beer. On this we managed an excellent evening, enjoying a first class cabaret floor show and getting up to dance every time the waiter hovered near by!

An amusing incident happened while Joan and I had absented ourselves to the powder room. At this time both Harry and Fred sported luxuriant black beards, somewhat unusual in 1956 when beards were not in general fashion. A middle aged Englishman slightly inebriated, went up to them and said "Excuse me gentlemen, but you don't often see two at once (referring to the beards) Where do you come from? Are you off a ship?"

Fred looked at him very seriously and said in a conspiratorially whisper "I am afraid I can't tell you that".

The Middle aged Englishman immediately dropped his voice to a whisper and replied " That's quite all right, I understand" touched the side of his nose with his finger, and went unsteadily off, smiling happily, probably convinced he had just met a couple of Russian spies!

Apart from this encounter, the general atmosphere in the room was very much more formal than at the Sea View Hotel, but we found Raffles an elegant and excellent hotel of the Old Colonial style. Another accident took place outside the front of the hotel while we were there and the shaken victims were brought into the foyer of the hotel.

We did not forget the children's entertainment and one afternoon was spent along with our friends and their children, daughter Celia who was about the same age as Jennifer and her three brothers, at the Singapore Swimming Club. A vast place that included restaurants, retiring rooms, lounges, balconies, a hall that enclosed two water gardens, fish pools and of course a huge Olympic sized pool with diving boards, plus another large children's pool. Both our girls were regular water babies after two years in Malaya and thoroughly enjoyed their afternoon here. When darkness fell a film show in the open air was provided for the children and although Jennifer managed to keep her eyes open Virginia fell fast asleep on my lap.

One morning was spent visiting the Raffles Museum. Jennifer at eight years old was at an age when everything was interesting, Virginia three years younger again preferred the natural history section with its stuffed animals and birds, with just a small word of approval for the model houses and boats. The museum was too extensive to see all in one morning and unfortunately our time in Singapore too short to pay a return visit as there was so much to see and do.

Haw Par Villa was one of the sights we had to see. Known also as Tiger Balm Gardens it was started by a wealthy Chinese who had made his money from the Tiger Balm ointment, a cure for all ills in that part of the world. He had been told by a Fortune Teller that as long as he continued to build, he would continue to live. So he started building these fantastic gardens as a sort of memorial to his ancestors. That is the story as we heard it and I believe he was still alive and still building at the time of our visit.

The gardens were full of grottoes housing highly coloured plaster figures in the form of animals, humans, and creatures of fantasy, some lovely, some comic and some frankly horrific. We skipped as many of the horrific ones as possible showing terrible scenes of torture with all the gruesome details and tried concentrating on the pretty and the comic, but we had some difficulty in drawing Virginia away from a tableaux of fearsome gorillas exposing their fangs at passers by. Other areas of the garden had attractive pagodas, bridges, fishponds and streams, the whole gardens covering many acres.

Luckily this form of eastern culture appeared to have no ill effects on the girls and we suffered no nightmares.

We were very comfortable in the Grand Hotel at Katong that catered especially for families with children, providing amahs when required, flexible meal times and a large garden with lawns and swings. When the Chinese amah came to stay with Jennifer and Virginia on the evening we were out, she brought her palm leaf woven mat which she spread on the floor at the end of the girl's beds and spent her watch time there. The hotel was right on the sea front and had a small beach. Unfortunately our four-day stay soon came to an end and we had to pack for our return journey to Penang.

At the time of our stay, Singapore was still a city built mainly of Colonial style buildings roofed with red tiles or green domes, but there were signs of things to come. Where some of the tallest features had been the church spires, or the tower of the Victoria Memorial Hall, these were now being overshadowed by the new skyscrapers of buildings, such as the Bank of China and the Asia Insurance. On the domestic front tall blocks of flats of ten to twelve storeys were taking shape. Old China Town still existed with its narrow alleys decorated overhead by the long bamboo poles on which the washing was hung out to dry from the crowded tenement buildings on each side.

The busy, colourful and noisy Chinese Peoples Market that took place at night by the glare of thousands of bright neon lights and the more subtle glow of pressure lamps and burning stoves of the many and various food stalls, was an ideal place to savour the tastes and aromas of Chinese fare. Here at night it was possible, to eat, drink, meet your friends and find entertainment, but you could also get a haircut, shave, or do your weekly shopping. Here it was possible to see women in Sam Foos, the pyjama like costume with traditional Hair styles carrying baby in a sling on their backs, as well as the modern young woman in western dress with short permed hair. In contrast to the modern young lady one occasionally saw old grey haired ladies tottering along on bound feet, a relic of the days when women were less free. Children joined their parents in the bustle of the market and seemed not to suffer from late nights and irregular sleeping patterns.

Not far from this busy market were the Chinese Death Houses. It was here that many old people came to die. Death was accepted and waited for with calm resignation. The relatives of the recently deceased accompanied by their children sat around tables placed outside the death house accepting donations of money from friends that I assumed went towards the cost of the most elaborate funeral they could afford.

Change alley was a well-known place in Singapore where it was said bargains could be bought. We paid a visit and bought a watch cheaply, only to discover it did not work, so no bargain as far as we were concerned!

Leaving Singapore at 8.30 in the morning we re-crossed the causeway to Johore and retraced our road to Muar having been warned against the alternative road to Seremban due to renewed CT activity. A short break for lunch at the Rest House and then on to Malacca. From Malacca we took an inland road and spent the night at Seremban. Our journey from Singapore to Seremban covered around 220 miles and was quite easy until on almost reaching the outskirts of Seremban we were hit by a terrific rainstorm. The rain descended in a blinding sheet of water. Some drivers gave up and pulled in to the side until the storm passed. Our windscreen wipers worked at double speed enabling us to keep going albeit at much reduced speed.

The Seremban Rest House was excellent both in appearance and service. It was positioned overlooking the attractive Lake Gardens. Situated in the gardens was a small museum contained in a beautiful Malay house built on tall stilts with attap roof and decorated with lovely and intricate carvings. The house had belonged to a Malay prince and had been purchased and moved to its present site by the Museum Organisation. The children enjoyed climbing its steep steps and exploring its cool interior.

Following the inland road on leaving Seremban we made our way to Kuala Lumpur without trouble and took a break for lunch at Robinson's Store. Another pleasant hour was spent buying Christmas presents to send home. In the Malayan Handicraft Shop we found great difficulty in choosing gifts from the many delightful artefacts they had on sale including batik cloth, jewellery, carvings and silverware.

This time my navigation on leaving Kuala Lumpur was better and we found our way to Rawang and our friend's house without entanglement in the one way traffic system and enjoyed a welcome cup of tea. However we had not left the storms behind and the first part of our journey from Rawang to Kuala Kubu Bahru was made in heavy rain. The rain ceased but had left its mark for at one section of the way we passed a spot where the road had caved in. There was a large gap, a void where the bank had collapsed. A detour for cars had been made and on this we drove.

Banks and hillsides frequently collapsed in the monsoon seasons due to the excessive rain and roads had to be closed. Some friends of ours were unlucky enough to be caught in such a landslide when travelling into the hills. They along with other vehicles found their way barred by a blockage of stones and earth and had left their car to see what could be done, when the bank above them began to move. Someone shouted a warning and looking up they saw the mass of earth start to slide. Everyone started to run down the road away from this looming mass as they heard the ominous rattle of stones and grinding of the soil as it gained momentum. Then with a rush it was upon them. Dick was swept off his feet by the branches of a tree brought down with the slide and brushed aside from the main path of its descent. Joyce was not so lucky; she was engulfed in the tons of mud, greenery and rocks that descended with the slide. When Dick regained his feet, Joyce was nowhere to be seen. An Indian driver who had escaped the avalanche shouted, pointed and raced back to the mass now covering the road. He had seen the top of Joyce's head among the mayhem and frantically dug with his fingers to free her from suffocation Dick and others joined him and between them managed to dig her free. Unconscious, badly bruised and cut Joyce was carried to an ambulance that was among the vehicles halted on the road. The ambulance managed to turn and make its way back to Batu Gajah hospital with Joyce and Dick. Although badly scared and shocked Joyce recovered from this horrifying experience, considering herself lucky to have survived.

Most of the rains came during April and August but varied in intensity. The occasional storm would also descend in other months, the wet and dry seasons were not as clearly defined as they were in Ceylon (Sri Lanka). The storms could be terrifying with great claps of thunder rolling in the heavens and blinding sheets of lightening flashing across the skies one after another with barely seconds intervals.

Motoring back home one evening Harry and I were trying to follow the road, our vision obscured by the torrential rain when a tree ahead of us suddenly appeared to disintegrate in an explosion of blue flame. Shaken but luckily unhurt we continued on our way, concerned and anxious to return to the children whom we had left in Zenna's care. All was well, the children asleep and blissfully unaware of the world raging around them.

The electric storms could be spectacular if your nerve was sufficiently strong. The lightening produced many vivid colours and shapes far excelling the most magnificent of all firework displays.

Once more out of the rain and on into bright sunshine we drove into the small town of Kuala Kubu Bahru, usually referred to as KKB. KKB is situated at the beginning of the pass road through the mountains known as The Gap that leads to the hill station of Frazers Hill and on to the East Coast.

The Rest House here was very small, only three bedrooms, but each a chalet type with its own bathroom and sitting room. A young army couple were staying in one of the rooms, and we took the other two. The children were thrilled at having a little house all to themselves. The Rest House was quite new and very clean and comfortable. The food was excellent. Our evening dinner consisted of asparagus soup, roast pheasant and vegetables, and lemon soufflé with meringue, all beautifully cooked and delicious to eat. The servants, a Chinese man and his wife, were very pleasant and helpful and although they spoke very little English, we were able to understand one another with their bit of English, my bit of Malay and a lot of sign language.

They told us that the night before we had arrived the Rifle Brigade had shot two terrorists only a mile away from the Rest House. This action accounted for the activity of many army patrols we had noticed on route. On our journey from Seremban to Kuala Kubu Bahru we had passed through the village of Semenyih where a patrol had recently killed the number two Terrorist, the fellow who was second in command of the CTs after Chin Peng, the overall leader of the Communist Terrorists in Malaya.

On the whole of our return journey we saw patrols in jungle green going into or coming out of the jungle. In a letter written to my parents at the time I wrote " There are very few incidents by CTs now and their numbers are decreasing rapidly due to security patrols and the increasing surrenders."

In October, November and December 1955 an attempt to negotiate peace and form an amnesty was made by the Malayan Government headed by Tenku Abdul Rahman. Terms were handed to Chin Peng's envoy at a meeting that took place in the small town of Klian Intan in the state of Perak not far from the border with Thailand. These terms were considered and rejected by Chin Peng in November who sent his own terms for negotiation to the Tenku. A further meeting was arranged to take place at Baling in Kedah for December. The Conducting Officer was John Davis who was then District Officer at Prai and Butterworth and whose daughter was one of Harry's pupils. John Davis had been one of the members of Force 136, who being landed at Pankor Island, made his way through the country then occupied by heavy forces of Japanese troops to join with Chin Peng and other Communist fighters to carry out guerrilla warfare from their jungle camps. He knew Chin Peng well in those days so was accepted by him as an intermediary.

In spite of all efforts the talks reached an impasse, Chin Peng declaring "We will carry on the struggle to the last man". The Tenku saying "I will never give in….. So you must give in". Hence the war continued.

Our journey also continued from KKB towards Ipoh along winding roads. Due to an early start we saw a number of rubber tappers at work in the plantations adjoining the road. With their sharp knives they were making a slanting cut into the trunks of the trees and fixing cups to catch the latex. They did this about 8am and then about mid-day they visited the trees again to empty the cups that by then were full of latex into two large pails carried by a yoke across their shoulders. These pails were then taken to a collecting point and emptied into big churns that were conveyed to the factory. Rubber was sent to Britain in two ways or forms, one, as rubber sheets and two, as liquid latex in large tankers.

In my letter home I wrote of a meeting. "At Slim River we came across three RAF Regiment trucks parked by the roadside. Who should be standing beside one of them sten gun in hand, but a friend of ours from Butterworth named Pete Hill. We stopped to have a little chat and collect a message for his wife before he went off to his firing practice and we continued on our journey" My letter goes on "At Ipoh we stopped long enough to have a drink and buy some curry puffs and sausage rolls to eat and pressed on once more. We ate our lunch as we drove out of Ipoh, but had not quite finished it by the time we reached the Black Area. As you are not allowed to carry food in restricted areas, I guiltily hid the bag out of sight every time I saw a policeman!"

From KKB to Ipoh was supposedly a White Area, I say supposedly, because we had seen many active patrols and it was obvious that some terrorists had managed to re-enter the area. With such difficult terrain to police it was impossible to guarantee absolute safety.

Although we had no time to explore properly, we could see that Ipoh was a fair sized town of broad roads with a busy shopping centre. Promising ourselves to come back and take a further look another time, we pressed on towards home. Another 110 miles brought us to Butterworth and a couple more to the ferry terminal. Here we found a long queue of lorries, cars, bicycles and passengers waiting in the hot sun, their Chinese or Indian drivers were making the most of the opportunity for a short nap. I envied them their ability to drop of to sleep within a few seconds of closing their eyes and ignore the world around them. They seemed to remain oblivious and recumbent until the ferry docked when they slowly unfolded and leisurely took their turn to drive up the ramp and board the vessel.

The angle of the ramp was dependent upon the state of the tide at the time. It could be reasonably level and simple to drive aboard when the tide was at moderate height. On the other hand when the tide was low so was the ramp and one drove downhill. The most difficult time was when there was a very high tide and one drove steeply uphill. On one such occasion the steering wheel almost parted from the steering column on our Wolsey 680 as we took the incline and Harry had to ram it sharply back into place. Luckily momentum carried us safely aboard and saved us from a dip in the ocean. The ferries were frequent. As one pulled out another drew in and after seeing two of them leave we were able to embark on the third. Vehicles were guided and closely lined up by members of the ferry crew, but enough space was allowed for passengers to leave the vehicles and walk on the deck if they wished. It was a chance to cool off in the pleasant sea breeze for the 10-15 minutes it took to make the crossing.

Penang or Georgetown was a free port so there was no stop for customs officials on our way home, as there had been required on the commencement of our trip to the mainland. Within a few minutes of landing we were back once more in our flat where we found Zenna waiting to greet us with a welcoming smile.

Outside the Mosque Alor Star

Mosque at Alor Star

Main trunk road to Alor Star

Rest house on Maxwells Hill

On Maxwells Hill

Police armoured car at check point

Kampong School

Harry stops for a chat by the roadside while the family stretch their legs on the seashore. On the way to Malacca

Malacca town centre

St Pauls church. Site of St. Xavier's grave and old dutch tomb stones

Rest house, Malacca

Spinning tops

Ferry at Muar

The girls find Chinese playmates at Batu Pahat rest house

Raffles Hotel, Singapore

Haw Par Villa, Singapore

Haw Par Villa, Singapore

CHAPTER TWELVE

Moving to Our Third Home in Penang

Our holiday over, we next had to concentrate on our imminent move into a new flat. While we had been absent Zenna had spring-cleaned our present apartment leaving everything spick and span for the next tenant. In writing home to my parents I said "We actually moved in on my birthday that makes the second year in succession...... My birthday was not forgotten, Harry gave me a gold watch and the children gave me a black lace fan. Another pleasant surprise I had was a bunch of flowers from Yvonne in the next flat and a bottle of Channel No.5 scent."

Our new flat in Ayer Rajah Road was far more comfortable, spacious and in a quieter area. It was brand new, partly furnished and had its own entrance and garage. Previously we had shared a common entrance and staircase with 5 other apartments that often caused noise and confusion on the stairway. Now we had not only our own front door, but stairs and hallway as well, the floors to this area being tiled and floors throughout the rest of the flat were wooden parquet and were simple to clean. The living room was large and airy, having an air- flow from windows on two sides, one with folding doors leading onto a balcony. There were two bedrooms, each with twin beds and each room having a wide window and another door with another small balcony. Each bedroom had its own bathroom that delighted our girls who had visions of glorious games to play at bedtime. A study, well fitted kitchen, amah's room and bathroom made up the rest of the interior, and a large balcony over the two garages of our flat and the neighbour's downstairs completed the apartment for which we paid 425 Malayan dollars a month.

In the compound in which our new home was sited were six flats altogether in three buildings, well distanced from each other, all identical and each containing a ground floor and upper floor apartment. The buildings were designed by the son of our Chinese

Landlord, who was studying to be an architect. We thought he had done a good job and still thought so after living in one of them for over two years. The only item he had forgotten was a doorbell to inform us of callers. From the living room area it was impossible to hear anyone knocking at the door. As our contract with the landlord forbid us to put any nails or screws into the structure of the building, we requested the landlord's agent to arrange to have a bell installed. In due time this was done for all the flats.

One of our RAF neighbours and his family from Kelawei Flats in Northern Road moved into the flat opposite us a few weeks later, so Virginia and Jennifer still had their friends nearby. Even our cat Ching seemed pleased with the move. All tenants in the other apartments were European, for the flats had been designed to suit European lifestyle. Several of our neighbours worked in Penang's commercial life as rubber brokers or bank officials. One neighbour was an ex-nurse who had suffered imprisonment in Changi during the occupation by the Japanese and below us lived a young Army Officer with his wife and baby daughter. When they later moved on, a RAF officer and his wife, a teacher moved in.

Adjacent to our compound was a large Chinese house and garden that was patrolled by huge Pincher Doberman dogs and on the other side was a house inhabited by an Indian family. The Towkey (landlord) was responsible for our drive and surrounding lawns. To keep these in order a Kebun or gardener came each week, bringing his two goats. The kebun sat in the shade while his goats cropped the grass. Who needs a lawn mower?

Some problems were caused by stray dogs. Numbers of them roamed the streets at night in packs, raiding the dustbins, awaking the householders with the clatter of falling lids and bins and the snapping and snarling of dogs bickering. The strewn mass of rubbish that met our eyes in the morning was a continual nuisance. With the help of the landlord we were able to find a bin that the dogs were unable to open and so at least resolve the problem of the rubbish. We could do nothing about the dogs themselves whose barking set off all the dogs in the neighbourhood and gave noisy nights, but eventually we became so accustomed to the sound that we were able to sleep though it.

Although there was a free RSPCA clinic in Georgetown few of the local people used it. Instead of taking unwanted animals to be dealt with in a sensible way, kittens and puppies were often dumped by the side of a road to take their chance with the traffic, or left outside houses where European people lived. Jennifer and Virginia along with other children were frequently bringing in kittens they had found outside. Sometimes we found homes for them, but if that was not possible we took them to the clinic otherwise we would have been overrun with animals.

Ching did not take kindly to these new additions, no doubt feeling his position was being usurped. One little kitten we took in was in a sorry state when the girls found it. Thin and terrified it had even had its whiskers cut. The girls were determined to care for it. They found a box for it to sleep in and encouraged it to feed and generally gave it much attention. Ching watched these ministrations with a baleful eye and spat at the kitten whenever it came near. The kitten never retaliated in any way, wanting only friendship and peace. As the small scrap gained in strength we gave it its own feeding dish alongside Ching's placed on the kitchen floor near the stove. One day both animals were drinking from their bowls side by side, when Zenna put some food into hot fat to fry. There was a tremendous hiss as the food met the fat and Ching jumped into the air, took a startled look at the kitten and fled the room. He obviously thought that the worm had turned and the kitten was retaliating at long last. The kitten lapped on unconcerned.

Our move to our new home was celebrated by a house warming to which we invited neighbours and friends including the landlords of our first Chinese house in Clove Hall Road, a charming Chinese couple. A catering firm provided a splendid array of 'Kitchi Makan' (small food) items, vol au vents, pate slices and other delicious and attractive buffet style and easy to eat food, to which I added dishes of fruit and desserts. The company was as attractive and delightfully assorted as the food. They represented several different nationalities including Chinese, Siamese, American and Dutch, but all conversed in English and even the hosts found it an enjoyable and pleasant evening.

Malaya proved to have a very busy social life for most expatriates. Working hours started early in the morning and continued during the cooler hours of the day until about 12.30-1p.m. We had a light lunch and then came the hottest and quietest period of the day when most people took to their beds for an hour or two. Zenna went back to her village to her cool attap house until about 3.30

when she returned to make tea and prepare the children's evening meal. Most activities of a physical kind began from around 5pm. as the sun began to lose a little of its heat and it was possible to fit in a game of badminton or golf before darkness descended. Once night had fallen and the air comparatively cool, the restaurants, shops, and places of entertainment in town became thronged with customers. The small Chinese and Malay portable stalls were wheeled into the most advantage positions and with charcoal burners and paraffin lamps aglow the stall holders prepared to serve the population through much of the night.

Visits to cocktail parties that usually started around 6p.m. dinner parties, dances held by various organisations to celebrate special occasions such as St. George's Day or other national days, Battle of Britain Ball, and balls in aid of various charities, others held by commercial firms combined with formal receptions at the Residency or Services headquarters of Army and Airforce all combined to keep many expatriates extremely busy. To begin with we took great pleasure in dressing up and joining in these social activities, for the ladies had ample opportunity to array themselves in beautiful gowns and jewellery. Glamorous short dresses for cocktail parties and flowing long creations for balls. The men looking distinguished and smart in their dinner jackets of white sharkskin or other materials. Delectable food, a wide selection of drinks from which to choose, all available with the minimum of effort on our part. Bearing in mind that we had left Britain in a state of austerity where on teachers pay we could not afford to buy butter or ham, coming to such a life in Malaya was like Alice coming into Wonderland and finding all the rules had changed.

It may seem difficult to believe, but after a time these bright social occasions began to pall and we grew tired of the same small talk and even of some of the faces we saw time after time in a relatively small community. Gradually we withdrew and declined some invitations and instead held small intimate dinner parties at home opening up a wider circle of chosen friends from varied positions in the Crown Colony and mainland. We still retain good friends from this period of our life, friendships that have lasted over many years and distances.

Many of the invitations sent out for various occasions were more in the form of a social duty expected of people of a certain office or standing. I shall never forget one coffee morning I went to soon after my arrival that was given by the senior Wing Commander's wife of the RAF Station. Seating was arranged in an approximate circle in the comfortable living room of this officer's quarters. Once all were seated coffee and biscuits were brought in by the amah and houseboy and dispensed by the lady of the house. Most of the guests already knew one another well. My hostess introduced me and my immediate neighbours in the circle engaged me in friendly conversation. I was just beginning to feel at ease and enjoy the chat, when after fifteen minutes the Wing Commander's wife looked at her watch and said "All Change"! At this command to my amazement, the ladies all rose to their feet and moved to another chair in a different position in the circle. This happened every fifteen minutes and cut short a number of promising conversations. I found it all most amusing, if a trifle distracting.

Sunday lunch was a frequent popular informal social occasion. The lunch was usually a curry buffet and guests were invited to help themselves from a table on which mounds of fluffy, white rice stood alongside bowls of steaming beef or chicken curries whose delicious aroma permeated the air. Attractive smaller dishes of all kinds of sambals added colour to the spread, pineapple, paw paw, chillies. Chutneys, coconut, cucumber, nuts and bananas were only some of the variety offered from which to flavour your meal. Jugs of clear water were also provided to cool the palate, but if you were a wise and seasoned curry eater, these were left untouched until your meal was finished, otherwise the heat engendered by the curry felt much greater when only a fireman's hose seemed able to put out the fire!.

Providing a novice approached their first curry with caution the sensation could be extremely pleasant, particularly so in the case of Malay curries that generally included a large amount of fruit. However, I did have to ask Zenna to stop using my saucepans for making her curry as we were not quite up to her strength of taste and all our normal meals started to arrive with a strong curry flavour.

On some evenings we met up with one or two friends to enjoy a meal at one of the Chinese Restaurants in town. A popular rendezvous was the roof top restaurant of the Peking Hotel where it was possible to enjoy the cooler breezes of an elevated position and also watch the activities of the busy thoroughfare of Penang Road taking place beneath us. Night seemed to bring a magical quality to the town. Any scruffy or unpleasant aspects were hidden from sight and instead the highly coloured lights of neon signs so loved by the Chinese businessmen blazed and flashed from hotels, cinemas and shops. Head lights from cars, lamps from trishas, glowing lights from pressure lamps and charcoal fires from street side stalls, along with the street lamps that lined this bustling main road of Georgetown sparkled and shone in the world below us. In the distance the lights of Penang Hill twinkled. From this height five floors up sounds were muted and harmonised into a symphony of life.

All the family developed a taste for Chinese food particularly Harry whose favourite dish at that time was Bee Hoon, a thin vermicelli like noodle with a mixture of prawns, pork, vegetables and sauces. Most of the dishes or recipes we had in the restaurants in Penang were from the Hokkien Chinese and so varied slightly from the mainly Cantonese Chinese of Singapore. An invitation from Chinese friends to an evening Makan (Malay for food or meal) proved interesting. The meal took place at a popular night club named, 'The Green Parrot'. The night club restaurant was positioned on the coast a short way out of the main town. In front of the main building a wide concrete area projected over the sea in the form of a large balcony. On this balcony were placed a number of large circular tables each surrounded by as many as twenty chairs. The whole area being illuminated with coloured lights strung between upright poles around the balcony and on the building itself.

Groups of people, mostly Chinese already occupied some of the tables, but it seemed an extra large table had been reserved for our host and his guests, a party of twelve altogether with about equal numbers of Chinese and Europeans. Our meal started with small bowls of soup of a moderately thick consistency and pleasant taste that may have been crab. I was relieved to find it was not sharks fin or birds nest soup, both of which are expensive delicacies, but to my taste revolting. On the one occasion I tried them it was like eating unpleasant clinging glue. I was therefore glad I did not have to offend my hosts by leaving my soup.

While we ate waiters continued to come carrying dishes containing a variety of foods that were placed in the centre of the table on a revolving 'Lazy Susan' arrangement. Our soup bowls and spoons were removed and a fresh bowl and chopsticks provided and from then on it was up to the guests to help themselves. Luckily we had been getting a little practice with our chopsticks both in the privacy of our home and with the children when we went out for a Chinese meal 'en famille'. Although by no means perfect we were at least proficient enough to pick up some of the larger pieces of food and convey them to our mouths without dropping too many on the way. The single grain of rice however, was still beyond our capabilities and so we concentrated on those foods we could manage. I noticed that some of the Chinese guests held the bowl close to their mouths when eating some of the more difficult ingredients.

The general mode of eating was using your chopsticks to take food from the large central plates, dip it into one of the many smaller dishes of varied sauces dotting the table and then still maintaining a light but steady grip with your chopsticks, pop it into your mouth. Chicken, crab, duck, pork, fish, oysters, bamboo shoots, sweet corn, mixed vegetables, rice and mee were all eaten this way. In all there were fourteen different courses, but naturally one only ate a little of each. Harry was guided through the meal by a charming young Chinese girl who picked out for him what she described as the best pieces; the real delicacies. From the large whole fish (ikan) she picked out pieces from the head and from the whole suckling pig that was the highlight of the meal, she took the cheek. The crackling on the pig was cut into small squares, crisp and delicious, making it easy to pick off with chopsticks. The crackling was eaten before starting upon the meat. I was told it used to be customary for the richer families to eat only the crackling and the meat was then given to the servants of the house.

Chinese households were often large and complicated, containing many relations apart from the nucleus of a family, as westerners knew it, husband wife and children. Some of the Chinese households we were introduced to included parents, in –laws and possibly cousins or widowed relations. To fathom out who was who could be a problem for a simple westerner.

At a table behind us, a group of Chinese men without wives were enjoying their evening. There was much laughing and talking and as their meal progressed so did their drinking. Every so often one of their party stood up, raised his tumbler of brandy crying "Yam Sing" to which all replied in chorus "Yam Sing" and drained their glasses. A very merry bunch by the end of the evening!

Our meal was concluded with dessert of various kinds of fresh fruit and then thick black coffee. After this if you were so inclined there was a small dance floor on which to gyrate or sway as the mood took you, to the strains of Hawaiian type music of the soft, gentle kind played by a small band, that combined with the quiet motion of the ocean was easily capable of lulling one to a peaceful sleep under the influence of a balmy breeze and beautiful night sky filled with countless stars.

The children were not forgotten. There were many parties they attended or held, but what they enjoyed most was going to the beach or swimming pool and some evenings when we invited friends to join us for a beach barbecue. On those evenings we found a quiet sandy cove where we set up our little portable burner buckets into which we put our charcoal and when it was smouldering nicely out came the pan and sausages to cook and sizzle on the grill. Swimming costumes were the only dress and the children revelled in the freedom and space, climbing the rocks, somersaulting on the sand or splashing in the sea, a child's dream of paradise. When energy was expended there was the appetising thought of those sizzling sausages to eat.

On one or two special occasions they were allowed other late nights when we took them to New World Park. New World Park was a vast amusement area, but an amusement park minus the gaudy machines of pin-tables and one- armed bandits that we in the west have come to associate with such places. In the 1950s New World Park was a place of entertainment by people for people and each night it was thronged with men women and children of all ages and all races meeting their friends to enjoy a few hours away from work and worries. In this busy but relaxed atmosphere, one could choose to watch the Chinese Opera; or a puppet theatre; an Indian film; take part in a Malay ronggeng dance; simply wander among the many stalls sampling the varied foods or buying some of the cheap and colourful nick-knacks offered by the vendors.

Every stall or booth was illuminated by coloured light bulbs, or glowing stoves and the whole area vibrated with the sounds of music, vendor's shouts and happy laughter. All the different languages and dialects of the inhabitants of Malaya could be heard in New World Park and other parks such as this throughout the country.

The Whole family found the Chinese Opera a place of strong

fascination. It was held in a booth of wooden structure of thirty feet or so in length and twenty feet in width, of which three of its sides were open to public view above waist height. Under this structure, rows of crude wooden benches were placed before the raised stage on which the performers played their parts. The plays performed were mostly of time honoured tales which the audience, or at least the Chinese members of the audience knew by heart. The actors were dressed in the elaborate costumes of the traditional Chinese Opera, brightly coloured with much sparkling decoration. The make up was also traditional and gave their faces a mask like appearance. The good and bad characters were sharply defined by the basic foundation of the make up. Good characters having a white mask while the bad characters had red. Features such as eyes and eyebrows, were accentuated giving actors faces an unreal, puppet appearance. The singsong speech of the actors was emphasised on gong and cymbals struck at frequent intervals by a man dressed in an old vest and khaki shorts standing at the side of the stage.

Other distractions included the stagehands, also dressed in old vest and shorts, who continually moved around behind the performers changing the props and scenery as one scene evolved into another. The Operas would last for several hours, but we were able to view over the theatre's surrounding wall and once the children had had their fill, move on.

The tune 'Cherry blossom pink, Apple blossom white, vividly recalls for me the memory of the Malay ronggeng dancers on the roofed and raised platform in the World Park. On this platform around a bare wooden rectangular dancing area sat a number of brightly dressed Malay girls in their attractive sarongs and kabayas and chiffon scarves their gold earrings, necklaces and bracelets reflecting the light from the bare electric bulbs above them. These girls were the taxi dancers of the dance place. Should a man wish to dance he must first buy a ticket that he was then free to present to any of the girls sitting around the floor. On receiving his ticket, the girl would then accompany the man for one dance. The dance finished she would return to her place. In ronggeng there was no touching of the dance partners. The man set the steps, sometimes using a handkerchief or scarf that he waved to accompany his movements to the tune of the record or occasionally the musicians, being played at the time and the woman did her best to follow him. Together the dance was usually one of gentle flowing grace. There appeared to be little verbal communication between the two and the taxi dancer appeared to be as impassive in her expression when she finished the dance as she had been when she had begun.

The puppet theatre was a great attraction for our children. Usually they were Chinese puppets on the Punch and Judy style of show with the puppeteer hidden in his booth manipulating the characters above a shelf. Sometimes we saw the Malay shadow puppets 'Wayang Kulit' in which the intricate buffalo hide flat shapes of the puppets were projected on long rods behind a canvas screen in front of a lamp. In this way the puppet shadows were seen by the audience sitting in front of the screen. The 'Wayang Kulit' performed traditional tales taken from legends based on old Hindu epics. The puppet operator works from a bamboo platform sitting behind the screen. His finely cut and often vividly painted puppets close at hand. Sometimes the puppeteer's performances were accompanied by Malay musicians to add emphasis to critical points of the story.

Jennifer and Virginia loved these outings and when their excitement and interest finally had to give way to drooping eyelids and yawns we took them home and tucked them into bed to contentedly sleep and dream.

The Queen's birthday celebration in June was a much more formal and ceremonial occasion that the whole family attended. This was a day in which the hats came out. Most women in Malaya never wore a hat except on the occasion of the Queen's Birthday Parade and on that day women searched the backs of their cupboards or in their trunks to find the hat brought out from Europe, wrapped to protect it from cockroaches and other unpleasant creatures and kept for this one special day.

Seats were allocated around the Padang and all had to be in their places by 8.15a.m. when the Resident Commissioner dressed in his official uniform with plumes waving from his tropical helmet and carrying his ceremonial sword arrived to take the salute. In towns where there was no Resident Commissioner, the senior official would do the honours. The parade of service men, police and other groups marched past the officials and guests to the music of the regimental bands, while the Resident Commissioner took the salute. It was a stirring sight.

30A Ayer Rajah Road. The upper flat

Picnic on the beach

Queen's Birthday Parade, Townhall, Georgetown, Penang, June 1956

Queen's Birthday Parade, Townhall, Georgetown, Penang, June 1956

Queen's Birthday Parade, Townhall, Georgetown, Penang, June 1956

CHAPTER THIRTEEN

Holiday in Sri Lanka

In August 1957 we took advantage of the concession flights for those working for the RAF and decided that we would try to take the children to Ceylon renamed Sri Lanka when gaining independence. The country held happy memories for Harry and I, since it was in Ceylon that we worked and first met during the war.

We took a chance, packed a couple of cases and went over to Butterworth to wait for the plane from Singapore bound for Negombo, Ceylon. Luck was with us. Four people got off at Butterworth to spend their leave in Penang , so we took their places on the plane to Ceylon. There were about twenty passengers altogether. The plane was a Bristol Freighter and not exactly comfortable, but since the trip was free we could not complain. Being my first trip by air, as it was for the children, we were a little apprehensive as we fastened our safety belts for the take off, but all went well and we were soon airborne, looking down on the jungle clad hills of Penang and then the open sea.

About 12 a.m. we were given lunch boxes to still our appetites and about 2 p.m. we landed at Car Nicobar, a tiny coral island with only the air strip to give it any importance on the map. Here we saw a native village of bamboo and palm leaves huts built on stilts and under one of them we saw a captive fruit bat. A man from the village demonstrated how they hunted with bows and arrows.

We took off again after about half an hour during which time the plane had been refuelled. Then came the most trying part of the trip. The noise in the plane was loud and continual. It was too loud for conversation with the person seated next to you. Most people read, but we had omitted to take any books with us and so did our best to try and sleep.

It became very cold when we reached an altitude of over 6,000ft.

Luckily Harry was able to get our cardigans from the cases without much trouble. Soon after leaving Car Nicobar we were told to put our watches back two hours. The trip was extremely boring and uneventful until, just as it was getting dark we crossed the coastline of Ceylon. Then we ran though a storm that bumped the plane around somewhat and caused Jennifer to be sick. Harry looked after Jennifer whilst I kept an eye on Virginia, but she, tough little soul was perfectly happy playing cards. After a while I began to feel a little upset inside; luckily we flew into calmer weather just in time to save my dignity! We were then able to look down on the ranges of hills and the rivers and roads running through them, just as if we were looking down on a large- scale map. Here and there we could see lights and fires burning and knew there must be small towns or villages there. We had to fly through one more short storm before we landed, and ten hours after leaving Butterworth we were all heartily glad to get out of the aircraft at Negombo.

The RAF Air Movements Officials met us there and took us to the transit mess where we were allocated rooms for the night. Not one of us felt like eating, so had the boy bring us a large pot of coffee and hot milk for the children. The children were in bed and fast asleep before the milk arrived, so Harry and I drank it and then tumbled into bed ourselves.

We all slept soundly and were awake at five thirty next morning ready to start the next part of our journey on the train.

The train journey became a little complicated as we had been misinformed as to details of time etc. What we did was to take a very hectic taxi ride from Negombo to a small town named Regama to catch the 7.27 a.m. train . The station was extremely dirty and ill-kept and we had a job to find the booking office that we finally discovered in a hole in the wall. The train came in on time, but on boarding it we were informed by the other occupant of the carriage that we should have to change trains after about fifty miles at a station with a very long name beginning with P and there we must wait one and a half hours to pick up the train which left Colombo at 9 a.m. We could have saved ourselves a lot of trouble if we had gone direct to Colombo from Negombo, a distance of about twenty- five miles. Still the interesting conversation we had with our carriage companion made our extra journey worthwhile. He was a Burgher, or Eurasian descended from the early Portugese settlers and a lawyer by profession. He was a widely travelled man having journeyed over quite a slice of Europe, Australia and America.

There was a reasonable if not inspiring waiting room at Polgehawela that we shared with the curious stares of the local population. Obviously Europeans were rather rare creatures in Ceylon in those days. There was a book stall with English magazines and books that helped to prevent the children from becoming too restless. Eventually the train pulled into the station drawn by one of the diesel engines presented to the Ceylon Government by the Canadian Government as economic aid under the Colombo Plan.

Sharing the first class compartment this time were several Europeans and Asians, One of the Europeans was a Post Office expert from England with his wife, sent to Ceylon under the Colombo Plan to give advice on the postal organisation. Another occupant was a Japanese, loaned to Ceylon, who was testing the vibration of the carriage with a little machine. He was a railway expert. Most of the other members were holiday- makers like ourselves all bound for the hills. One family had just finished a contract in India and they were visiting friends in Ceylon before returning to England.

As the train climbed we began to get the most glorious views of the countryside. The flat padi fields gave way to terraces on which every inch of space had been cultivated and which gave the impression of great flights of steps mounting the hillside.

At one o'clock we had lunch on the train. The Sinhalese waiters were most courteous and helpful but the food was of poor quality, the water was warm and the table linen stained and in shreds. (The general standard seemed to have deteriorated all round in the last ten years. I feared the same thing might happen in Malaya after Merdaka.)

During the afternoon we came into the tea growing area and saw the hillsides covered with the small dark green tea bushes, shaded by larger trees planted among them. Most of the tea factories we saw were well kept buildings and on the whole the tea plantations gave a neat and tidy appearance. The higher the train climbed the more extensive and breathtaking the views became.

We reached Diyatalawa at 5 p.m. and took a taxi to our destination that was a bungalow about two miles from the station.

The bungalow was large and airy, and the children were delighted with the garden that included a swing and a see-saw. They also discovered a table-tennis room within the building. We were high on the slope and had beautiful views across the valley to the next range of hills.

Some of the buildings and layout had been changed since Harry and I spent our first holiday together there in 1945, but we were able to locate various landmarks that we remembered. Ella Camp, where Harry stayed and the leave centre where I stayed had both been taken over by the Ceylon Army. The children enjoyed watching the recruits at their drill on the big football ground.

During our stay in Diyatalawa we met one or two of the native 'boys' who had worked in the leave centre in 1945 and had a chat with them. The Navy had then left Ceylon. Everything was gradually closing down and the local native civilians were finding it difficult to get jobs.

The day after our arrival we went on a trip to Dunhinda Falls. We travelled by coach along hair raising roads of continuous S-bends, whose edges dropped away hundreds of feet below us. I never did have a head for heights and knowing the fatalistic attitude of the drivers of this country from a previous experience when the wheels of the truck in which I was travelling skidded and stopped short; just six inches short of a precipice, I was frankly terrified. I only hope it did not show! Our transport finished twenty two miles from Diyatalawa, but then we discovered it was necessary to hike a further one and a half miles along mountain foot paths, some of which were very narrow with a nasty drop if you missed your footing, before reaching the actual waterfall.

The Guide led the way with Jennifer and Virginia matching him step for step and although I endeavoured to keep up with them, Harry and I were left well behind. The children were already dabbling their feet in the pool when we saw them again. The falls were roughly six hundred feet high and I should imagine that in the rainy season are quite awe inspiring, but when we saw them there was not a great volume of water although we still felt the spray from about thirty yards distance. We had been warned not to bathe in the pool at the foot of the waterfall as there had been several deaths due to treacherous currents.

We had a stiff climb back to the road, arriving in a very hot and sticky state. Harry bought a fresh pineapple and had the young boy cut it into quarters that we shared between us. We found it most refreshing. On our way back to Diyatalawa we passed through the town of Budulla that is the terminus of the railway line from Colombo to the hills.

We visited a second waterfall the following week. It was near the small town of Koslanda and named Diyaluma Falls. Again the fall was not as spectacular as it would be during the rainy season, but the breeze was blowing the water into a gossamer spray, glinting in the sunlight and dropping to the rocks six hundred and twenty eight feet below. Harry and I had visited these falls in November 1945 during the rainy season when there was a solid looking sheet of water reaching the edge of the main road. This time the foot of the fall was a good thirty yards from the road. Harry and I remembered a rubber plantation opposite the falls through which we walked and incidentally collected a couple of leaches on our ankles trying to take the short cut. We removed them with the lit end of a cigarette. The rubber trees were still there but in a very neglected state. The latex was no longer tapped and collected and the undergrowth had become a jungle of tangled weed. Watching from the car window we passed several acres of rubber trees all in the same condition.

The whole family became very keen on nature study during our holiday, having plenty of opportunity to watch the birds and animals at close range. There are an amazing variety of coloured birds, differing in size from tiny brightly coloured Flower Peckers to the huge black, noisy crows. We had seen a group of four Kingfishers with beautiful green backs and red heads diving from one of the trees in the garden to the water tank and back to the tree again. Several of the birds have most distinctive calls that we grew to recognise, especially the little black and white Fantails who woke us every morning as they practised their little scale slightly off key. Other fascinating little creatures are the chipmunks or tree rats. They have a bushy tail like a squirrel that sticks straight up in the air when they run on the ground. One little fellow used the electric cable slung between the buildings as a short cut from tree to tree and gave the impression of a tight- rope- walker.

There is a range of hills in this part of Ceylon that is called 'The Sleeping Warrior' because outlined against the sky they give a clear silhouette of a sleeping man, from the forehead, nose and chin down to the toes. It is most remarkable.

There were two house-boys working in the bungalow and one cook. Each 'boy ' has a Christian name. Our two were Henry and Alan. Henry had been married five months. He and his wife had a padi field and his wife was the owner of twelve bullocks, which made them comparatively wealthy. Alan had been in the Royal Navy for ten years and seen quite a bit of the world. He was then considering joining the Ceylon Navy, but the Ceylon Navy had only a small number of ships and far more recruits than they could cope with at that time. The house-boys worked from six a.m. to ten p.m. with breaks in between, for two rupees fifty cents a day.

One morning we took a taxi into Bandarawela, a small town about four miles distance from the bungalow. We walked through the narrow streets lined with the typical open fronted shanty shops, taking our own cine film. We watched the silver-smiths at work, admired the stacks of shining brass pots, gazed at the colourful local vegetables, trying to guess how they would taste and bought some beautiful red carnations in the local market. When asking the price of the flowers, I was told "Twenty five for one rupee Lady". But I was completely fooled, for instead of counting each stalk as I had expected, he counted each small bloom even to the half- open buds, and there were as many as four or five on some stalks! However we reached a compromise and left one another satisfied with the bargain.

The time came to break off from our sight seeing and refresh ourselves with a pot of coffee in Bandarawela Hotel where Harry and I had spent some happy hours dancing twelve years before. It was a delightful long low building set in attractive gardens where there were aviaries of budgerigars set in the shade of some beautiful spreading trees. The children were fascinated by the birds. The coffee was excellent but we appeared to be the only people there apart from the house-boys. We spoke to the elderly house-boy who wore the horseshoe shaped tortoiseshell comb in his hair, a custom denoting he came from a high caste family and had never carried burdens on his head. This custom was fast dying out and was only seen amongst the older men. We were told that in the whole hotel of about forty bedrooms, there were only eight guests! We spoke with him of the war years and his opinion was that "those were the days". Business had sadly declined since then.

Virginia had a wonderful time doodling on the hotel writing pad. She certainly left her mark there!

Another morning we paid a most interesting visit to a tea factory. Craig Plantation was owned by a European firm, and we noticed the great contrast in the condition of the bushes to those on the other side of the road which were locally owned; badly neglected and of poor quality. We were driven all round the plantation by the manager in his little Morris Minor. It took even the steepest slopes without trouble. The Manager told us the story of tea from the bush to the crate for export.

Briefly the pickers pick the bud and first two leaves on the stems of each bush. These are sent to the factory and put on canvas racks called tats and left to wither for eighteen hours. Then the withered leaves were fed through chutes into machines called rollers that rolled the tea around to rid it of any further moisture. It was then passed through a sieve to another rack and left to dry again for three hours. From there it was passed though a hot air conveyer belt system that removed any final moisture that might still remain. After this the tea was graded. This was done by using machine and hand sieves that removed the dust and separated the tea ready for the crate. It all seemed very simple and to produce the tea ready to drink from the actual picking takes roughly twenty four hours. We were invited to try the different flavours strained into labelled bowls set out in the manager's office.

The manager entertained us in his bungalow afterwards. This was situated in a high position with a most wonderful view of the countryside and had a delightful garden with sweeping green lawns. The bungalow itself was comfortable and spacious.

We were informed that of the eleven hundred labourers the estate employed, ten hundred were Tamils and one hundred Sinhalese. Most of the labourers would probably spend all their life on the estate. They were provided with good housing, medical attention, schools for their children and their own churches in which to worship. We were invited inside their new Hindu temple. This was very clean and the figures depicting the various gods were very gaily coloured.

The European planters in 1957 were no longer allowed to take their profits out of Ceylon, and only allowed to take twenty per cent of their provident fund with them when they retired.

Since in my previous stay in Ceylon I had never succeeded in visiting Kandy I was determined to take the opportunity on this occasion. Harry and I decided that we could afford to spend one night there. We had had a small motel recommended to us, that made a reasonable charge.

The train journey took five hours and it was very noticeable that on the last part of the journey as we came nearer to Kandy the railway stations became progressively cleaner and of course less smelly. Some of them had attractive flower- beds displayed around the station and potted plants suspended from the roof. We passed through Perydenia where there are some excellent botanical gardens within easy reach from Kandy. Unfortunately our time was so limited and the weather so uncertain that we were unable to see them. As soon as the train pulled into Kandy our bags were grabbed by two unshaven ragged individuals who marched towards the exit leaving us to follow with the tickets. Safely outside the station our luggage was thrust into a small and extremely dilapidated taxi whose driver was obviously a personal friend of the luggage carrier and not ours! With a great deal of spluttering and back firing from the engine we set off down the main street in the direction, we hoped, of the Peak View Motel where we intended to spend the night. Strange as it seemed to us we arrived safely at the motel that was situated about two miles out of town on the road to the Kattagusta River.

The Motel was pleasantly modern, very clean and our bedroom was quite comfortable and large enough to accommodate two extra beds for the children who preferred to stay with us. The Manager and staff did everything they could to make our brief stay an enjoyable one. They were most understanding where the children were concerned.

Retaining our ancient taxi as it was the only one available, we asked the driver to take us to the Kattagusta River where we hoped to see the elephants bathe. The ride was nerve racking and somewhat hard on everyone's backside due to the springs having lost much of their original bounce and the very rough road along which we travelled. We suffered twenty minutes of this before reaching the river. The river at this point was about one hundred yards in breadth and we were told its muddy waters emptied themselves into the sea at Tricomalee.

Almost before the taxi had stopped a dark faced gentleman in white dhoti and jacket carrying a walking stick was opening the door and ushering us out. 'Tourists' must have been written all over us as the Chief Mahout, as the gentleman turned out to be, immediately called up the mahouts and their elephants who had been bathing in the river. There were five elephants altogether, three adult and two young ones. Although we were told these were working elephants they were well trained in their circus tricks that they performed to an admiring audience and thus made a very nice sideline for their mahouts. The elephants worked through the morning shifting and hauling heavy loads of timber, then in the afternoon providing there were no tourists of course, they were allowed to relax in the river, cooling themselves, by blowing great fountains of brown water from their trunks. Rolling in a muddy river occasionally dousing his companions appeared to

be the elephants idea of paradise.

One of the animals was commanded to kneel and Jennifer and Virginia were placed upon its back, the Chief Mahout having first spread his silk handkerchief on the elephant's thick grey hide. When we asked Jennifer "How does it feel up there?" She replied very shortly "Wet!" That was understandable. When Harry had positioned himself in a suitable spot to film, Jumbo proceeded to walk towards him. The front view was quite dignified but from where I stood behind the group the whole affair seemed most comical. The hindquarters of this massive beast rolled from side to side and so of course did Jennifer and Virginia. A rumba for three!

Having been relieved of all our change under ten rupees, we climbed into our bone- shaker taxi and left to the accompaniment of yells from the Chief Mahout who obviously was under the impression that he had been cheated of his full dues.

We very thankfully paid off our taxi driver on our return to Kandy, a journey not without hazards, including many strange noises and jerks issuing from the realms of the so called

Engine. All of us sat tensed on the edge of our seats expecting the whole contraption to blow up at any minute.

Badly in need of relaxation we entered the Queens Hotel for a cup of coffee. The Queens was another vast hotel with its many empty rooms echoing through lack of customers, at least that is how it appeared to us. There actually seemed to be twice as many House boys as guests.

The Hotel is close to Kandy's beautiful lake, a shimmering sheet of water set among lush green hills. Kandy is the setting for the great Pera-hera. The procession of decorated elephants, one of which carries the sacred relic, the tooth of Buddha, in a small casket on its back. The elephants are accompanied by equally highly adorned Kandyan dancers and drummers who perform their agile and rhythmic cavortions along the route of the procession.

Unfortunately we missed the great occasion by a few days, but we could at least see Dalada Maligawa the famous 'Temple of the Tooth' where the relic is housed. The small Pagoda-like shape of its main entrance was familiar from the many pictures we had seen and with a helpful guide we were able to climb the steps leading up from the road and through the doorway in the walls of the main building. We could do no more than glance in at the rather dark bare entrance room as scaffolding had been erected all around in order that repairs could be made to the fabric of the building. However we visited one of the other Buddist Temples in Kandy, and saw the sacred Bodhi tree that spreads its heavy branches over the courtyard of the temple and its long tapering leaves are hung around the roofs of the shrines. One of the yellow robed monks gave us two leaves to keep and which, we were assured would bring lasting happiness. Along the roadside near to the temples were stalls laden with the lovely waxen, white flowers of the Frangipani whose exotically heavy scent filled the air and mingled with the heat, dust, the smell of charcoal fires and other indefinable odours to give the tang of the Far Eastern tropics. These beautiful flowers are offered to Buddha at the shrines by his devoted followers.

Leaving the smooth bell shaped domes of the temple we made our way past the long low building of the museum that in former times was the palace of the kings of Kandy, and returned to the motel to prepare for our journey back to Diyatalawa.

One bright and sunny morning we decided to visit the town of Nawara Eliya, the holiday resort of the hills. We were warned we might find it rather chilly there so packed our cardigans in our basket and caught the 8 a.m. train. The train climbed steadily from four thousand feet to over six thousand feet at which height we ran into heavy cloud, wet and very cold. We left the train at Nanu Oya station and took a taxi into Nawara Eliya. It poured with rain the whole of the day and had been like this for the past three weeks. It seemed so strange that Diyatalawa only thirty miles away was experiencing a near drought whilst here we found raging torrents in rivers and water to spare.

It was here that I noticed the quaint way in which the local population carried their umbrellas when not in use. The umbrellas were furled and hooked into their jacket collars and allowed to hang down their backs like a thick black pigtail! You might compare it to the way a city man hooks his umbrella over his arm when he wishes to read his newspaper. After seeing this I understood why the old fashioned black umbrellas were so popular. Obviously the modern type without the hook handle would be no use at all!

In the hill towns the men were fond of wearing brightly coloured scarves around their heads, which reminded me of crowd supporters of the popular football teams in the United Kingdom.

The cold and rain were so persistent that we found it necessary to spend some of our cherished rupees on raincoats and long woollen socks for the girls. We bought these in Cargills, one of the larger European shops in Nawara Eliya. Whilst I saw to the dressing of the children, Harry had a long chat about cameras to the manager of the shop who had noticed the movie camera Harry carried. The three turret Brownie Kodak we had was completely new to them in that part of the world although it had been on sale in Malaya for the past two years. The manager showed us the single lens Kodak movie camera he had on sale and asked us the price we had paid for our camera. We were amazed when we discovered that due to import tax, the single lens model he showed us cost in Ceylon four times the price we paid for our superior model in Malaya.

Harry had wanted to climb Mount Pedro up which there is a comparatively easy footpath to the summit at eight thousand feet, but due to the bad weather we could not see Mount Pedro, let alone climb it!

The Grand Hotel still stood facing the golf course. Harry spent a leave there in 1944. We went in to buy the children some books from the bookstall there, and stayed for an hour intrigued by the fascinating display at the jewellery shop. The shop offered some of the wealth of Ceylon, silver and gold and precious stones glowing and gleaming from every shelf. Some of the heavy jewelled collars, bangles and hair comb pins of old Ceylon were on display to our dazzled eyes. After turning down rings and brooches worth hundreds of pounds, we bought a silver filigree brooch in the form of a butterfly and a moonstone brooch set in silver. I am afraid we left the assistants very disappointed men.

The Grosvenor Hotel has left an indelible mark on our memory, not because of the lunch we had there, although it was an excellent meal, well cooked and plenty of it, but because there we saw our very first orange tree laden with its brightly coloured fruit.

After lunch it was time to make our way back to Nanu Oya station to catch the three o'clock train. Unfortunately the train was late and we had to spend a very uncomfortable half- hour trying to keep warm and avoid getting wet. We had forgotten that one could feel so cold especially in the Tropics. There was no reasonable waiting room on this station so Harry and I played games chasing Jennifer and Virginia up and down the platform to keep them moving whilst the local population huddled up in their saris and dhotis, stared at us in amazement. The sunshine and warmth of Diyatalawa felt very good to us on our return.

Wednesday was the great day in Diyatalawa. It was Market Day. On one of the hillsides a large square was wired off with barbed wire and here very early in the morning the vendors gathered from the surrounding countryside and squatted within this square with their wares spread around them. Soon the customers were flocking to take their pick of the goods displayed. There were the products of the market gardens to choose from, many different varieties of vegetables and fruit that the vendor weighed on scales suspended from his hand. Or perhaps a new pot was needed for the family and chosen from the rows of red earthenware pots that the potter offered for sale. Then there was the man who offered a variety of goods, from gaily coloured, glass bracelets the women loved to wear to the cheap and gaudy plastic toys for the younger members of the family. Always there was a crowd of women around the vendors offering attractive lengths of cotton material or perhaps some chiffon with which to make a new sari. The candy stall was the favourite with the children as it would be in any country. For a few cents they could buy brightly coloured pink fudge or vivid orange sweets, sorted by hand and wrapped in a piece of the local newspaper.

There were no longer any of the tourist attractions to be seen., Such as handbags and slippers made of leopard skin, and there was very little of the Kandy silver-work available, although the latter was in plentiful supply in the towns frequented by tourists such as Nawara Eliya, Kandy and Colombo.

By eleven thirty a.m. the market place was clear, vendors and buyers alike having packed their goods into the family bullock cart or simply piled them on the heads and gone on their homeward way. A few days later it was time for us to collect our baggage together and leave these wonderful hills.

On our return to Negombo calamity befell us. We were unable to get an aircraft to Malaya for another week and had to arrange to stay in Negombo. That same night, I was woken by Virginia crying out. When I went to comfort her I found she had a raging fever.

Throughout the night she continued with high fever and sickness. When the doctor arrived she was taken into the RAF hospital and dysentery was diagnosed. For the following week she was in isolation, although we were allowed to visit her every day providing we kept our distance. Fortunately, with the good care of the nurses and doctors Virginia soon began to show signs of improvement and cheerfully revelled in all the attention she attracted from the staff as the only child patient in the hospital. No other member of the family contacted the disease and I feel that it was Virginia's habit of sucking her thumb that was the cause of her illness.

Without her sister's company Jennifer looked for other amusements. She was delighted to find many of the tree rats were quite tame and would come down from the Kadjan or palm leaf thatched roof to feed from her hand. On one occasion one little fellow over reached himself and losing his grip on the veranda roof landed on Jennifer's head much to the surprise of them both.

The village of Negombo was not far off and early one morning the three of us took a taxi to go and watch the fishing fleet come in. By the time we arrived many of the boats were in and the large nets were spread over the wide sandy beach to dry. As we watched we saw many more frail craft with their square brown sails make their way through the heavy surf, at times almost disappearing in the troughs of the swelling waves.

We had to admire the skill of the fishermen as with the aid of their long bamboo poles they guided their catamarans safely to shore and pulled them onto the sand. There the women and boys disentangled the fish free from the nets and dropped them into the waiting baskets of woven palm fronds. The women then balanced the baskets on their heads and made their way to the nearby market where the fish was immediately sold.

On another day we paid a visit to Colombo, the Capital town of Ceylon or Sri Lanka as it now is. To see the Clock tower with its lantern top was like saying "Hello " again to an old friend. The tower stands astride the street leading to the sea front promenade. Its light is a landmark for shipping in the area and its arch a popular meeting place in town. Taxis had replaced the rickshaws of former days although a few could still be seen.

After the quiet and casual life of the hill towns and villages, the capital seemed all a bustle, its streets full of business men and administrators clad in white shirts and trousers rather than the skirt like dhotis that were every day apparel in the hills.

We felt the humidity of this coastal area close upon us and were glad to find a cool café and enjoy some iced tea. Refreshed we wandered in and out of the shops in the main street. I was particularly attracted to those selling beautifully embroidered saris. Each sari measures six yards in length and provides a most graceful garment for the equally graceful woman in this part of the world. The best saris are so fine that they can be drawn through a wedding ring and the embroidery is exquisite. I do not know whether this still applies, but in 1957 I was told the making of these saris was still a home industry and each weaver could be recognised by their own distinctive designs.

The lace makers with their lace pillows and bobbins were no longer to be found squatting in the shady colonnade working with deft fingers. Instead there were women with cheap brown suitcases filled with lace mats, tablecloths and edgings doing their best to persuade us to part them from their wares. Somehow the brown suitcase failed to attract in the way the tools of the craft were prone to do. However I bought some lace mats that are still in use today.

One great change we noticed in the town was the absence of the beggers. As a profession it seemed to have declined, at least they were no longer to be seen in the streets. Ten years before it was impossible to walk anywhere in town without being constantly pestered for your loose change.

The rest of our time was spent wandering around among the attractive buildings, imposing but un-fussy in their architecture with arched windows and cool colonnades. We visited the port area and saw the liners and merchant vessels riding at anchor in the wide harbour and memories of my first arrival in Ceylon from a troopship in 1945 flooded back to me. The same large black crows were still scavenging about the docks, completely unconcerned by the movements of humans. Their audacity had always amused me.

With Virginia's continuing improvement we were able to make plans to return to our home in Penang and at the end of the week early in the morning, we collected Virginia complete with bottle of medicine and took her straight to the aircraft. Then came another ten hours of unremitting buffeting of our ear drums relieved only by the half hour refuelling stop at Car Nicobar and finally our safe landing at Butterworth.

It had been an exciting and apart from Virginia's illness, enjoyable holiday marred only by one disappointment, tragic in the eyes of one member of the family. Somewhere on the trip Jennifer had lost her Teddy bear. Old he may have been and even battered, but he was her dearest love and sorely missed. Teddy, wherever you may be, you are not forgotten!

The train on a bend in the hills to Diyatalawa

Padi field terraces, seen from the train on the way to Diyatalawa

In the hills, view from the train on way to Diyatalawa, Sri Lanka

View of the countryside from the train, Sri Lanka

A tricky corner on track to Dunhinda Waterfall

Dunhinda Waterfall, Sri Lanka

Dialuma Falls, Sri Lanka

Harry and Jennifer studying 'The Sleeping Warrior Hills', Diyatalawa. Sri Lanka

Brassware shop Bandrawhela Sri Lanka

Virginia with carnations at Bandrawhela, Sri Lanka

Bandrawhela Hotel, Sri Lanka 1957

Managers bungalow on tea estate, Sri Lanka

Tea Pickers, Sri Lanka

At the tea factory, bowls of tea ready for tasting to check the quality, Sri Lanka

Hindu Temple built by the workers on the tea estate

Close up of carving on Hindu Temple, Tea Estate, Sri Lanka

Working elephants showing off their tricks by the Kattagusta River, Sri Lanka

Jennifer and Virginia enjoy a ride

The market, Diyatalawa, Sri Lanka 1957

Market trader weighing nuts, Diyatalawa, Sri Lanka

The potters, Diyatalawa Market, Sri Lanka

The Candy Man, Diyatalawa Market

Sri Lanka. Water Buffalo near Diyatalawa enjoying a bathe in a puddle

Negombo Beach. The fishermen spread their nets

The bungalow. H.M.S. Uva Diyatalawa. Sri Lanka

CHAPTER FOURTEEN
THE EMERGENCY

Although the Chinese Communist members had fought the Japanese alongside the British and Malay fighting forces in the jungle gurilla war, on the surrender of the Japanese at the end of World War II, the political members of the Chinese Communist Party, turned on the British Administration in an attempt to drive them out to enable the Chinese Communist Party to take over the country of Malaya.

In 1951 the British High Commissioner Sir Henry Gurney was murdered in the small town of Tras. The whole population of the town were moved and resettled elsewhere and the town of Tras shut down for five years.

The terrorists continued to try to spread their communist belief among the Chinese, particularly among the young members of the communities, encouraging the people to join them in their camps among the jungle. Those who resisted were killed. They preyed upon villages for food and weapons. During the Emergency ninety-four Planters were killed in attacks on their rubber or tea estates. A window in St Mary's Church, Kuala Lumpur is dedicated to them.

Britain sent forces from Army and RAF to fight the CTs and drive them from their hideouts. Forces from Fiji, Australia, the Gurkhas and others came to aid the British in their efforts. Many of the young men involved were young National Servicemen, recruited after 1946. The jungle at that time must have been a frightening place.

One RAF airman Sgt. McConnell lost in the jungle for three weeks, was found after being looked after by aborigines (Sakai) people. Another man, Driver Thomas Lee, in December 1956 was in a RNZAF Bristol Freighter that crashed on a mountain while on a mission dropping supplies. He was lost for 12 days. He had taken a survival course earlier that helped him, and although he had a broken ankle with the aid of a strong stake he cut, he managed to walk. He heard a 'voice' aircraft searching for him telling him to follow a stream and make for the river to wait for rescue. He ate raw rice and drank stream water and was found on the river bank by a search patrol.

Areas where CTs were active were named 'Black Areas'. Other parts of the country where the Government Military Police were in control and considered safe were termed 'White Areas'. There would be notice boards on the boundaries of all areas to inform travellers what sort of area they were entering or leaving.

I have already mentioned some methods used to control the CTs such as travellers being forbidden to carry food or arms through 'Black Areas' and the resettlement of people into 'New Towns ' for their protection. Other methods to encourage CTs to surrender were the 'Voice 'aircraft and dropping of leaflets giving an amnesty to those whom surrendered. Living on the run in jungle camps soon lost its appeal and many did surrender and return to their families. Processions of marching students carrying banners called upon terrorists to surrender, as did mothers who gathered together to appeal to their sons and daughters to give up the terrorist way of life and return home.

Efforts for talks between CT leaders and representatives of the Government had been made for many years. In October 1955 there was another attempt when Tenku Abdul Rahman sent terms to negotiate peace to Chin Peng the leader of the Communist Terrorists. There was a conference at Baliney, Kedah. The conducting officer for the Government was John Davis, the District Agent for the Butterworth area. He had fought along with Chin Peng against the Japanese occupation. Unfortunately Chin Peng rejected the government terms and submitted terms of his own that the Tenku could not accept.

In a message to the people of Malaya given at Kuala Lumpur on 12th November 1956, Tenku Abdul Rahman tells the terrorists " I wish to make it abundantly clear that the Government and the people of Malaya are supremely confident that the M.C.P. (Malayan Communist Party) will before long receive its death blow……..and that we are determined to fight the MCP until it is destroyed and terrorism is utterly stamped out."

The war still continued up until 'Merdaka' on 31st August 1957 when Malaya gained its independence from Britain. The promise of Merdaka encouraged some CTs to surrender, but some 'die hard'

areas did not give up until some time after that.
The casualties from June 1947- June 1957
M.C.P.
Total incidents- 20,841
Terrorists killed- 6,341
Captured - 1,236
Surrendered - 1,918
Wounded - 2.750
Security Forces, Police, Special Operational Volunteer Force and Kampong Home Guards.
Killed - 1,340, Wounded -1,585
Civilians
Killed - 2,456
Wounded - 1382
Missing - 807
Security forces came from many areas of the globe e.g. Australia, New Zealand, Fiji, E.Africa , Gurkhas and of course Britain.

In May 2008, I noticed a news item on the television of the Malayan Government presenting medals to servicemen who served in Malaya during the Emergency. It is good to know that their efforts have been remembered.

With weapons at the ready, platoon moves off through banana plantation on first round of Subang. They patrol perimeter watching any house which may have Red helpers

CHAPTER FIFTEEN

MERDAKA

Preparations for independence were under way in the 1950s and on January 1st 1956 Tenku Abdul Rahman, the Federation Chief Minister, left for London to meet Prime Minister Anthony Eden. He also met Lord Ogmore who was legal advisor to the Malayan Delegation. The Conference met at Lancaster House to deliberate on the future of Malaya. The Tenku also found time to meet Malayan students in London.

On February 8th 1956, an agreement was reached that promised 'Merdaka' Independence, on 31st August 1957 with full self-government and was signed by Tenku Abdul Rahman and British Colonial Secretary Mr Alan Lennex-Boyd. Four representatives of the Malay States Rulers also signed.

The Tenku was received by enthusiastically cheering crowds on his return to Malaya. Not everybody wanted or was happy about independence. There were some who would prefer to remain British Citizens and a large group who referred to themselves as the Queen's Chinese and were concerned that the new independent Government would be too pro-Malay.

Penang Island Colony, founded by Captain Francis Light, who was born in Dallingho, Suffolk, was the earliest British Settlement in the Far East and most people seemed happy and relaxed with the form of British Administration that had developed. If there were occasional outbreaks or riots, they were usually between hot heads among the young of the Chinese and Malay people, not against the British.

In a speech by the Minister of Commerce and Industry Dr. Ismail bin Dato Abdul Rahman said "the Malays must be prepared to rough it out after independence. They must get rid of any idea of a cushy time. Now you can always appeal to your British Masters for help when you are in difficulties, but when this country has achieved Merdaka you must be prepared to rough it out

145

yourselves."

The Chief Minister Tenku Abdul Rahman said that he had personally insisted that Malaya should retain expatriate officers even after Merdaka. "We have to keep them because many Asian officers have an inferiority complex and are asking for more time to take over key posts." He told 300 Kedah UMNO and Kaum Ibu members "We can drive them out at anytime, but this will only bring hardship to the country."

A Paramount Ruler from among the Sultans of the States was chosen. He was then elected to be the first ruler of the Federation of Malaya for a limited term of office. He was His Highness the Yang di-Pertuan Besar of Negri Sembilan who signed the Federation of Malaya Agreement 1957 on August 31st 1957. His Excellency Sir Donald MacGillivary High Commissioner signed for Britain transferring Sovereignty from the Queen to the Elected Ruler. The signing took place at King's House, Kuala Lumpur. As the clock struck Mid-night the new nation was born.

Celebrations took place on 31st August 1957 when 20,000 people watched the Federation Flag rise to the top of the flagpole in the Merdaka Stadium, Kuala Lumpur in a final act of the Independence Proclamation Ceremony. The Duke of Gloucester read a message from the Queen at the Proclamation Ceremony. "I have entrusted to my uncle the duty of acting as my representative at the celebrations of the Independence of your country. This is a great and memorable day for you; my thoughts and good wishes are with you as you take up the great and stimulating responsibilities of Independence; and it is with deep and real pleasure that I welcome you to the brotherhood of our Commonwealth family of nations."

"I am confident that Malaya will respond worthily to the challenging tasks of Independence and that she will continue to show to the world that example of moderation and goodwill between all races that has been so marked a feature of her history. May God bless and guide your country in the years that lie ahead."

The 20,000 stood to attention for the Federations new National Anthem 'Negara-Ku.

By October 1957 there were complaints in the newspapers that the only people who stood up for Nagara –Ku were the Europeans. "Since September 15 our National Anthem has been played at the end of each show at cinemas. It is disheartening to see that our ra'ayat do not have the National spirit. They ignore it and walk out"

At a handing over ceremony in Penang, the Resident Commissioner Mr R. P. Bingham, delivered the new constitutional instruments to Raja Sir Uda, first Governor of the new State of Penang, saying "This ceremony symbolises the culmination of the joint aim of Her Majesty's Government and all Malayans to achieve self government for this territory. I deem it a great honour to be present today to hand over this instrument. In doing so I wish the new State of Penang peace, prosperity and advancement in the future years as an equal partner with the other States of the Federation of Malaya."

The Large crowd greeted the proclamation with shouts of "Merdaka". As the band struck up the Federation anthem Negara-Ku, guns from the 105 Field Battery, Royal Australian Regiment boomed out a 101 gun salute. The Federation and Penang state flags were broken. Mr Bingham received the Union Flag when it was lowered for the last time from 182 foot flagmast on Fort Cornwallis at Penang Harbour.

On the 31st August in the brilliantly lit streets at night, crowds filled the streets of Penang as they celebrated the birth of their new State, some tears were shed as God Save the Queen was played for the last time. At UMNO headquarters in Macalister Road 2,000 members sat down to a sumptuous "nasi Merdaka" feast.

The next day's paper reported Malay girls and women shed their shyness to join in chanting thanksgiving prayer. Earlier in the evening the Federation and UMNO flags were carried round the island in a procession of cars. A religious leader Tuan Haji Riffaie blessed the flag. "It is up to the people to protect it, but it is Allah who will make it possible to protect it "he said.

Harry and I with the children walked into Georgetown to watch the celebrations and see the decorations in the streets. Archways in the shape of mosques covered with coloured electric bulbs spelling out " MERDAKA" were built across the roads of the town. People were happy and there was no animosity or violence of any kind and we and the children felt perfectly safe.

Next day was quiet. The newspaper reported "About the only activity was at post offices where philatelists jammed counters to buy first day covers."

CHAPTER SIXTEEN

Our last few months in Malaya

On our return from Ceylon (Sri Lanka) Harry had to open the new school term. I had resigned from my teaching at the Western Road School (Rhumah Hantu) as I intended to take the last few months of our stay in Malaya to prepare for the journey home, back to winter. I was able to see Virginia back to good health before becoming involved in other activities. As it happened, Harry was able to extend his contract an extra term to the following April as the new Head Teacher was not yet available. Many other commitments occurred during that time.

Harry and I were both keen singers and joined a choir and Penang Operatic Society. In January 1957, the Operatic Society had performed Gilbert and Sullivan's light opera 'The Sorcerer'. It was great fun to do and was performed to an appreciative audience. The papers reported "It cast a spell of delight". Members of the cast came from all parts of the community, civilians and service people combined, many of those playing leading characters were from RAF Butterworth. In the April of 1957 the choir performed the more serious works of "Handel's Messiah." Harry who had been a choirboy from the age of seven already knew the music by heart and loved it. I had to work harder to learn it as I had not sung it before. Again, the choir's efforts were appreciated by our audience.

Having left teaching at the Western Road School, my hopes of a more relaxed time to myself did not actually happen. Our friend Bob Bartos, who was head of the Army School Jennifer and Virginia were attending, found he was short of a teacher when one of his staff had completed her contract and went home. He asked if I could help until the new teacher arrived from U.K. So there I was back at work again for another term.

With the arrival of the Australian Forces in Malaya both RAF and Army Schools increased in pupil numbers. Harry at the RAF school found himself short of teachers in October of '57 when his two lady teachers were married in the same month. Once more I was called upon to help out and travelled with Harry on the ferry each day to RAF Butterworth. Instead of the year I had planned to prepare for travelling home, I managed only the last term when a new teacher was found for the RAF School.

Meantime, our friend Bob, Head of the Army School for four years, completed his contract and went back to U.K. Jennifer and Virginia changed school and went to the Western Road School where I used to teach. I had worked with the new Headmistress there who was also a friend.

The girls settled well in their new school and at last I was able to prepare for returning home to U.K. The main problem was to fit the family out with warm clothes for the great change of climate. The children of course having outgrown all the clothes we arrived with. A friend travelling as a Ship's Doctor on the liner 'Carthage', sailing between U.K., Penang and Hong Kong very kindly brought some warm but light Camel Hair cloth from Hong Kong for me. This enabled me to have overcoats for the children and myself made and a warm waistcoat for Harry. Other items, such as socks and stockings, I could buy from the bigger stores and shoes could be made by the local Chinese shoemakers, as long as I had a picture of what was needed. My mother and sister at home helped out by knitting jumpers and cardigans as Christmas presents for the girls.

Jennifer and Virginia were asked to be bridesmaids for the weddings of both of Harry's teachers and were delighted at the prospect. That meant that I had four more dresses to make and head- dresses as well, but as there were so many lovely materials available, I enjoyed the work.

Harry had written a pantomime with a part for every child in his school to perform in some way. He was kept busy with rehearsals and organising parents to help with costumes and scenery. The RAF service people were very helpful in providing such things. The younger classes gave a Nativity play. The pantomime 'The King Who Couldn't Laugh' and Nativity play were all a great success with children and naturally with their parents.

After the Christmas festivities, time flew by. We sold most of the furniture we had bought for our pleasant flat apart from the items we had bought for Zenna. We were allowed to carry a certain amount of goods home with us, but had decided to take the car as we were disembarking at Genoa, Italy and decided to drive home from there through Europe to show the girls other places before reaching England. Zenna asked if she could keep Ching, our cat. We agreed, glad that he would have a home with someone he knew.

Having made our farewells to friends and paid all bills, we packed our car and said our last goodbye to our Malayan home and to our kind amah and friend Zenna, before starting on our journey to Singapore and the ship back to Europe.

CHAPTER SEVENTEEN

Some Events of the 1950s

Many changes had been taking place in the world in the decade of the 1950s, some of which were to have long lasting effects.

1950

Britain's first self-service store, J. Sainsbury, opened in London

The musical Guys and Dolls had its premiere in New York.

Princess Ann only daughter of Queen Elizabeth II, was born.

The first episode of the radio serial The Archers was broadcast.

Listen with Mother started on radio, starting with the phrase "Are you sitting comfortably?"

Puppets Andy Pandy, Teddy and Looby Loo first appeared on BBC Television.

Senator Joseph McCarthy alleged that 205 communists were working in the US State Department.

1951

Winston Churchill became Prime Minister again just before his 77th birthday.

China forced the Dalai Lama to surrender control of Tibet's army and foreign affairs to Beijing.

During the Korean War, North Korean Troops and Chinese communists captured Seoul.

Jean Lee became the last woman to be hanged in Australia.

The Festival of Britain, intended to brighten the drab post-war era, was opened by George VI in London.

A TROPICAL ADVENTURE IN THE 1950s

1952

The video cassette recorder was first demonstrated in California

The liner United States made the fastest-ever crossing of the Atlantic, on her maiden voyage.

The first scheduled jet airliner passenger service began on a BOAC de Havilland Comet from London to Johannesburg, carrying 36 passengers.

Pope Pius XII declared that Television was a threat to family life.

Argentina's celebrated first lady Eva Peron died of cancer, aged 33.

1953

Jomo Kenyatta was jailed for heading the Mau Mau terror in Kenya Africa.

Nikita Krushchev became the First Secretary of the Communist Party of the Soviet Union.

The wedding of John (Jack) Kennedy and Jacqueline Lee Bouvier, later to become President and Mrs Kennedy of USA in 1961, took place.

Queen Elizabeth II was crowned in Westminster Abbey.

The Royal Yacht Britannia was launched.

The lavish musical comedy Gentlemen Prefer Blondes opened, featuring Marilyn Monroe and Jane Russell.

US athlete Jesse Owens set six world records in just 45 minutes.

Sir Edmond Hilary and Sherpa Tengzing became the first to reach the summit of Mount Everest.

1954

Food rationing ended in UK in July

The new Boeing 707 made its maiden flight from Seattle.

The first colour TV went on sale in the US for $1,000, about the same price as an automobile at the time.

Elvis Presley made his first and last appearance at the Grand Ole Opry, in Tennessee after a talent spotter suggested that he should stick to truck driving.

Roger Bannister became the first man to run a mile in less than four minutes.

An aerial search party found more than 100,000 people isolated from the world in Papua New Guinea.

A TROPICAL ADVENTURE IN THE 1950s

1955

Albert Einstein the physicist died in New Jersey, USA aged 76. His theory of relativity made the nuclear age possible.

The first McDonald's restaurant opened in San Bernardino, California.

Winston Churchill resigned as Prime Minister aged 80.

Victims of the US atomic bombing of Hiroshima arrived in America for plastic surgery.

Representatives from eight Communist countries, including the Soviet Union, signed the Warsaw Pact.

Ruth Ellis became the last woman to be hanged in Britain.

An advertisement for toothpaste was the first commercial to be screened on British Television.

Disneyland, the world's first theme park, opened near Anahelm, in California.

1956

Japan was admitted to the UN.

British and French Troops landed at Port Said, Egypt during the Suez Crisis.

Petrol was rationed in Britain in response to the Suez crisis and driving tests were suspended.

America dropped the first Hydrogen bomb over Bikini Atoll in the Pacific, devastating the island.

The first video tape was demonstrated in Chicago.

British Railways scrapped third-class travel.

The Eurovision Song Contest was first held in Lugano, Switzerland.

Prince Rainier of Monaco married Hollywood film star Grace Kelly.

A TROPICAL ADVENTURE IN THE 1950s

1957

Malaya became the last of Britain's major Asian colonies to gain independence as 170 years of colonial rule came to an end.

The European Community was established by West Germany, France, Italy, Holland, Belgium and Luxembourg.

The Treaty of Rome which established the European Economic Community was signed.

The winning design for the Sydney Opera House was unveiled.

Russia launched Sputnik1 the world's first artificial satellite. This was followed later by the Soviet satellite Sputnik 2. A Russian dog named 'Laika' was aboard and became the first traveller in space.

Agatha Christie's play 'The Mousetrap' became Britain's longest running play, reaching its 1998th performance.

1958

The first parking meters in Britain were installed in London's Mayfair. Britain introduced a system of marking yellow lines on roads, to indicate no-parking zones.

The USS Nautilus, the world's first atomic-powered submarine, became the first vessel to pass beneath the North Pole, emerging from under the 50ft thick ice after 96 hours.

Charles De Gaulle was elected the first president of the fifth Republic of France.

Belgium, the Netherlands and Luxembourg signed the Benelux Economic Union Treaty.

The state opening of Britain's Parliament was first televised.

President Eisenhower wished the world a special Merry Christmas- the first to be relayed via satellite.

Rock 'n' roll star Elvis Presley joined the US army for two years.

British singer Cliff Richard, 17, was signed to Columbia records.

1959

March, The Dalai Lama, spiritual leader of Tibet, fled to India from occupying Chinese forces. He was granted political asylum.

Indonesian President Sukarno dissolved parliament and assumed dictatorial powers.

Hawaii became the 50th state of the United States.

The Soviet spacecraft Lunik II was the first spacecraft to land on the moon.

Britain introduced the post code.

The first stretch of Britain's first motorway, the M1 was opened.

The Mini Car a symbol of the swinging sixties, was launched.

The Sound of Music opened in New York, starring Mary Martin

Acknowledgements to Eastern Daily Press.

A TROPICAL ADVENTURE IN THE 1950s

LIST OF ILLUSTRATIONS

A TROPICAL ADVENTURE IN THE 1950s